SONDRA LEE

I've Slept With Everybody
A Memoir

BearManor Media
2009

I've Slept With Everybody: A Memoir
© 2009 Sondra Lee

All rights reserved.

For information, address:

BearManor Media
P. O. Box 71426
Albany, GA 31708

bearmanormedia.com

Cover design by Leo Holder
Front cover photo by Julia Calfee
Back cover photo by Richard Heiman
All other images, except where indicated, courtesy of the author

Typesetting and layout by John Teehan

Published in the USA by BearManor Media

ISBN—1-59393-463-7

Table of Contents

Acknowledgements i
Introduction 1
Before the First Break 3
The First Break 5
High Button Shoes 7
After *High Button Shoes* 13
The Beginnings 17
The Catskills, or Mrs Ader's Walnut House on the Hill 21
Madame Alexandra Danilova and Other Teachers 25
Bando, Bindo, or Marlon Brando 31
Marlon, Others, and the Park Savoy 39
The First Time 43
After the Show 47
Louis Calhern 49
Lee Grant 51
Ben Hecht 53
Peter Pan 55
My Affair With France (and My First Affair in Paris) 67
Johnny Pineapple 77
Hotel Paradiso 79
A Guest of the Baron Philippe de Rothschild 85
Jean-Claude Vignes 87
Ballets USA – Spoleto 91
Gloria Swanson 95
Claire Bloom 97
Mouloudji, Mouloudji 99

The Beginning of the Baron and Me 103
Back to the Baron 107
One Night in the Sixties 111
The One and Only Billy Rose 113
Hello, Dolly!—Previews In Detroit 115
A Gift From Gower and Marge 117
Hello, Dolly! and Eileen Brennan 119
A Gift From the Star 121
Me and Ginger 123
More On *Hello, Dolly!* (or The Long Run) 125
Martha Raye: Vietnam 129
How I Met Fellini 131
Stella 133
After Capri, *La Dolce Vita* 137
On the Set of *Copkillers* and other 80s/90s Films 139
Larry Blyden 145
On Teaching 149
Sometimes It Happens 151
A Few Bumps in the Road 153
On Husbands 155
More on Relationships 159
On the Set of *Billy Bathgate* 163
Aging 165
From My Diary 169
Robbins Died at Twelve Noon 171
From the Corner of My Eye 177
A Life in the Arts 181
Last Words 183

Acknowledgments

A THRILLED SALUTE

I am truly grateful to my good friends who are still ever present in my life:

Tom Adcock, Corice Canton Arman, Bryan Bantry, Keith Baptista, Billie Becaul, Robert & Sallie Benton, Lois Bonfiglio, Patricia Bosworth, Kathy Brew, Oleg & Mirelle Briansky, Matthew Broderick, Jacquie Buglisi, Charles Busch, Julia Calfee, Terry Capucilli, Marge Champion, Gwin Joh Chin, Ron & Lynn Cohen, David Croland, Carmen de Lavallade, Diana de Vegh, Steve Downey, Alvin Epstein, Marisa Escribano, Barbara Flood, Jane Fonda, Saul & Patricia Gash, James Gavin, Billy Goldenberg, Bruce Goldstein, Joel Grey, Scott Griffin, Tammy Grimes, Roberto Guerra, Donna Hanover, Peter Harvey, Geoffrey Holder, Leo Holder, Joan Jett, Jennifer Joyce, Jay Julien, Kaoru, Willa Kim, Ilene Kristen, Angela Lansbury, Cyndi Lauper, Kevin Lewis, Bruce Lindstrom, John Buffalo Mailer, Norris Church Mailer, Anne Meara, Henry & Alicia Meer, Brian Mehan, Bill Merrill, Michael Mullins, Eric Myers, Mark Nadler, Nadya, Ben Northover, Maggie Paley, Sarah Jessica Parker, Georgina Parkinson, Dr. Joseph Porder, Phillip Quint, Klavdia Ramnareine, Bill Randolph, Philip & Marie Rhodes, Ned Rorem, Roy Round, Barbara & Ira Sahlman, Carole Shelly, Naomi Sorkin, Peter Stadlen, Elizabeth Stearns, K.T. Sullivan, Mickey Sumner, Kim Sykes, Peter Tate, Ghita Tazi, Wynn Thomas, Bonnie Timmerman, Amanda

Vaill, Harley Ware, Audrey Weston, Mark Zeller & Dana Alexis Zeller, Younis Zrikem, and especially Nancy Shayne, a most gifted and as-yet-unheralded composer, and Klavdia Ramnareine. And to Kathy Brew, who patiently helped shape and edit the amount of material I'd written, snatching time between her own film projects to get this together with me.

> I am honored beyond…*beyond*…
> – Sondra

My French Family

Linda Baron, designer; Asma Bastille, designer; Jean-Marie Besset, playwright; Madeleine Carbonnier, art historian; Julien Chatelin, photographer; Dr. Noel Chatelin and Elliott, educator; Marius Constant, conductor, composer; Andre Francois, painter and cartoonist, and his wife Margaret; Franta, painter; Stephanie Fribourg, actress; Arlette Gordon, filmmaker; Larry Hager, designer; Stan Kemper, playwright; Mary Kling, publisher; Ricky Leacock & Valerie Lalonde, filmmakers; Noel Lee, concert pianist, composer; Michel Legrand, composer; Tanya Lopert, actress; Fabienne Martin, agent; Fannie Paniez, writer; Jamie Bauer Paniez, producer; Monique Vigoroux, Picasso Museum, Valluris; Jean-Claude Vignes, painter, sculptor; Michelle Vignes, photographer; and Titine Vignes, artist.

Introduction

I AM IN AWE OF PEOPLE who save articles, reviews and photographs from the important periods in their lives. Most of my clippings and snapshots have been given to me by friends. Over the years, I tossed them carelessly into a cardboard box in my closet. Yet today, if I'm lucky enough to receive press and pictures, I hold on to them happily.

When you are young, you never think about holding on to things or that death is inevitable.

I enjoy looking at someone else's scrapbook just the same way friends like to examine my cardboard box filled with memorabilia, cards, bits of ribbon, a dried pressed flower, a compact with Mary Martin as Peter Pan etched on it, or Joe Layton's cigarette lighter.

Was it a gift?

I don't remember. But there it is.

I look further into my box. The edges of some of the photographs are bent or missing. Now as I peruse this cardboard corrugated wonder—which is so heavy I cannot lift it—I try to catalogue some of its contents. There emanating from it is an essence of must and mold, and a yellowing paper look that warns me to go gently and handle with care.

There are letters from Marlon Brando—my first crush, comrade, boyfriend. I read them and they are still sincere, silly and yet still mysterious.

What binds us? What mysterious element binds us with people? And how did I get here?

I will tell you.

Before the First Break

AS A YOUNG DANCER AT THE BEGINNING OF MY CAREER, people would always ask me the same question. "Are you Bambi Linn?" I'd be walking on 44th Street where the musical *Oklahoma* was playing and where Bambi Linn was appearing. Or I'd be coming from class on 56th or 57th Street. "Are you Bambi Linn?" After a time, there was no one I wanted to be more than Bambi Linn. So I would smile graciously and even sign her name in some person's autograph book and then make a quick getaway. Eventually, I was asked to audition for her part in the show, except I didn't get the job. "Not ready yet," is what they'd say.

A bit later, when a show called *Allegro* held auditions, I followed a group of dancers I recognized from various classes, changed into practice clothes as they had, and followed the waves of lines of dancers who executed a series of combination steps. I gathered that the choreographer was Agnes de Mille, the same one who choreographed *Oklahoma*. So I thought, "This is a sign." I'm always in pursuit of that sign.

Miss de Mille must have been intrigued a bit, and called me forward and began to ask me questions. I had been forewarned that whatever she asked I was to say "YES," so when she asked me who I studied modern dance with, I just said, "Yes, yes, yes."

"No dear, who?"

"*Who?* Who do you study with?" she asked again. The tape in my head was spinning.

I knew there was a Martha Graham and a Katherine Dunham. I planted my feet firmly and said, "Martha Dunham." Amused silence.

"Can you do a *swastika* or a *stag*?"

"Yes," I said with many teeth showing. Another amused silence as she waited.

"I tell ya what," I said. "Just come up here and do it and then I will, O.K.?" Muffled chortles from out front.

"That will not be necessary," she said. "Just join that group in the wings." And so I was chosen. We, the chosen ones, were brought out in a separate line and examined one by one. They then realized what I knew—I was much shorter than the other girls. So that was that. "Thank you, thank you very much," she said.

And I was dismissed.

The First Break

DEJECTED AND CONFUSED, I WANDERED down the street and started up Shubert Alley. I saw a group coming out of the stage door at the Shubert Theatre. "What's going on?" I asked.

"Well, we just auditioned for Robbins for *High Button Shoes*."

"Oh yeah?" I entered the stage door. It was empty and dark. "Who's Robbins?"

Out of nowhere this guy comes forward. "I'm Robbins. Who are you?"

"I'm Sondra, and I'd like to audition for this."

"The audition is over."

"Oh," I said, a bit humorously. "I just auditioned for *Allegro* and they found I was too short so they let me go. So I'm going home to commit suicide." A beat passed. There was a ring of truth in what I was saying and he caught it before I did.

"Don't go home and commit suicide, come over here and dance for me." I did. Then Robbins turned to someone taking notes for him. "Put her in group B. No, put her in group C. No, put her in Amazons." There was no trace of mirth on his face.

"Thanks, thanks a lot," I murmured humbly. I left my name and address—the 'ritzy' Park Savoy—and disappeared. I had no idea who he was or what had just happened.

A week went by. I received a card announcing the finals of *High Button Shoes*. I wasn't even sure what finals were but I went because the card told me to and I was flattered to be included. When I saw him, I waved and waved like Robbins was my uncle who was entering the country for the first time. At one point, we were given this little combination to do. The music was the type of bathing beauty music used in early movie musicals. We were told to go down to the waterfront, put our toe in the water and mime the words, "Ooh, it's cold." We had to do this twice. Then we had to, "Ooh, here comes my husband!" When my turn came I mimed the words but did a double take when I saw my husband. Everyone started to laugh and then applaud. I wasn't aware of why it had gone so well but it was a success.

After this, a heated discussion began between Jerome Robbins, the choreographer, and Monte Proser, one of the producers. After a few minutes I became aware that the discussion was about *me*. I inched closer, thinking they were going to make me into a star. Proser said, "But it will make eleven—and you can only have ten." Robbins said, "I want eleven." Proser said, "I don't want the kid with the…" I couldn't hear the rest. Then I clearly heard Jerry say, "Ten boys and eleven girls. I want the kid with the fat legs!"

Jerome Robbins had won. I was the kid with the fat legs!

So that's how I ended up in *High Button Shoes*. The kid with the fat legs was now a Broadway Baby. It also marked the beginning of my relationship with the genius of Jerome Robbins who graced my life for years. I still view him as a mentor and secret passion of my life.

High Button Shoes

"The Keystone Cop Ballet"

HIGH BUTTON SHOES WAS A SMASH HIT when it opened at the New Century Theatre on October 9, 1947. "The Keystone Cop Ballet" segment was inspired by the movies of Mack Sennett; the characters of Papa Crook, Mama Crook and Baby Crook were inspired from the cartoons of Charles Addams. It was the talk of the town and brought down the house every night. I was featured as Baby Crook. I was so new at this, so green, that often when the audience laughed at something I did, I joined them. (To this day I wonder why Jerry didn't kill me).

8 • I've Slept With Everybody: A Memoir

Vinnie Carbone (Papa Crook), Jackie Dodge (Mama Crook), and me (Baby Crook)

We began previews in Philadelphia. The score was by Jule Styne (*Funny Girl; Gypsy*), lyrics by Sammy Cahn (*Three Coins in the Fountain*) and directed by the one and only writer, actor, producer, and director—Mr. George Abbott. You could call everyone by their abbreviated names except for one—he was always Mr. Abbott. It starred Phil Silvers and Nanette Fabray and featured Jack McCauley, Joey Faye, Mark Dawson, Helen Gallagher, Donald Saddler, and Lois Lee (whose first name I would cover with my finger when pointing to the poster of the show and make believe it was mine).

While in previews, Jerry had me roll around on the pavement and in the alley of the theatre to dirty up my Baby Crook costume right before the show. He started to call me 'Peanuts' because he said I stepped right out of the Charles Schulz cartoon. I asked Jerry, "Which character?" He said, "All of them!" Peanuts remained my nickname for *years*. On the other hand, Mr. Abbott, the director, called me 'Cashew,' which seemed more refined. Still, it was 'Peanuts' that stuck.

I shared a dressing room with an elegant dancer, Jackie Dodge, who played the Older Girl in "The Picnic Ballet" and Mama Crook in "The

Keystone Cop Ballet." "The Picnic Ballet" was a tender story of unrequited love. It was painful, touching and inspired. An Older Boy (Arthur Partington) is in love with an Older Girl, but a Little Girl (played by me) adores the Older Boy. Jackie was a favorite of Jerry's. She went to society 'dos' and once came in sloshed for that night's performance. Thinking I would save the day, I tied my wrist to her wrist during part of the "The Keystone Cop Ballet." Mama Crook and Baby Crook are trying to escape from God-knows-what. Everyone is running in and out of doors and up and down stairs. A pier appears during the ballet which was about 8 to 10 feet above the crowd. At this point Baby Crook falls from the pier into the crowd. I realized that I'd have to fall backward to be caught below, but it took time to free my wrist from Jackie and the timing was off. I fell to the stage and almost caused a serious accident—I was knocked out cold!

Next thing I knew I was on a stretcher in the Baby Crook costume in the wardrobe room. Dr. Gundlefinger, the house doctor, (known as the 'killer') had been summoned. I jumped off the stretcher having no idea where I was going. I also forgot that I looked like a bald pinhead since my wig had fallen off and I only had a stocking cap on my head. I ran up the stairs into the wings and ran out on the stage before I could be caught and tamed. I had entered into a totally different part of the show. There was a jolted, confused look from the cast while the audience howled. And then Peanuts was gone!

Another time shortly after, I was intent on getting to the theatre as Jerry had decided to 'take out the improvements' we had all been guilty of adding. Suddenly, I was struck by a car. The driver jumped out, extremely concerned, as a trickle of blood ran down my forehead—but I had to be at the theatre. I think I actually apologized to him for hitting his car. I got to the theatre as quickly as possible, while pressing my head against my hand so blood would not drip on my beautiful costume.

At the memorial of Mr. George Abbott, which took place at the Majestic Theatre on June 5, 1995, Jerry Robbins was one of the speakers. For the first time, he spoke of the history of "The Picnic Ballet" in *High Button Shoes*. He had approached Mr. Abbott and told him that he created this piece but was not sure if it belonged in the show. Mr. Abbott replied he would take a look.

Indeed, Mr. Abbott was the director of *High Button Shoes* and Jerry was the choreographer. They retired to opposite sides of the theatre. Jerry

"Picnic Ballet," Arthur Partington and me

was terrified. We dancers had no idea of the stakes that were involved. After we had finished the ballet, Mr. Abbott told Jerry that he would be honored to have "The Picnic Ballet" in the show. When I heard him tell the story that day, I was moved and grateful. Mr. Abbott was gone, but I could still tell Jerry how much I loved him. I wrote a letter to him and received an equally loving reply.

What can I say about Jerry? He was a very sexy and mysterious person to me. His clothes were the work clothes of a dancer. Sweats, dark jeans, blue cotton work shirts, or a black or white sweater—always clean. His hands and his intense eyes were wonderful to observe. When his thoughts transferred into the movements he wanted, he often smiled or giggled. When he was not in a good mood, he turned as dark as the sky before a storm. The jaw would jut, the eyes became nervous and clouded over—you couldn't get in. Yet once you danced his movements and understood them—you never forgot the message, the story, the image. All of this has never left me. He told it his way and wanted it to be clearly represented as he conceived it. If you needed him to soothe your ego, look out—you could get skewered. It was better to just watch those ideas forming in his head. Where the inspiration came from was a miracle—the humor, the source of painful truths (which were often autobiographical)—all of this became his dances. He told it like it was. He was a shy person and although he never stuttered, when he became nervous his speech would falter.

He was open to the bone.

As time went by, he felt protected by his older women friends, especially those who treated him like a person and not like a cruel, demanding monster or a 'party' surprise. And when you followed Jerry's work, in whatever medium, you felt you knew him intimately. Although he failed me more than once when I needed him, I know I had also failed him at times.

Jerry loved simple things. He loved beautiful things. He was curious about most everything and did his homework. He also was happy just looking around in a supermarket or enjoying a good joke, a good poke, and a good hug just like the rest of us. He also happened to be a genius.

Years later, I was visiting Eaves Costume while being fitted for an outfit for a TV show. Something caught my eye.

Suspended from a bent wire hanger was my white dress from *High Button Shoes*—drooping and forlorn, without me in it. I loved the costume and wanted a piece of my life back again—a piece to examine—a time in which getting to the theatre for an early rehearsal was everything. I wanted to dance those dances again and perform every night. That entire way of living was bewildering, exhausting, joyful.

I had been given a gift and I ran with it.

Jerome Robbins and me

After High Button Shoes

AFTER *HIGH BUTTON SHOES*, I did the subway circuit version. We performed in vaudeville houses all around the country. It was the same show but restructured so it was just one hour. Most of the dialogue was removed, but all of the musical numbers remained. It was like a one hour mini-Broadway musical. We'd do it five to six times a day. That's right—*five to six times a day!*

We performed in huge theaters that housed big bands like Harry James and his orchestra or early Sinatra. There would be a stage show and a movie. It was unbelievably tiring. It took all the energy of a full-length show but it was much more compact. That was quite an experience.

I met Joe Layton, who would become a respected director, when we were playing at the Oriental Theatre in Chicago. The bad eating habits and stress of working those long hours took a toll on the dancers. There was one time Joe and I were extremely constipated. A helpful member of the company told us to get Citrate of Magnesia, which we did, and toasted one another in the dressing room. To us, it seemed a tasty drink until we hit the stage. Pure terror in our eyes as we passed one another. I whispered, "Joe, don't lift me!" As we passed each other again, Joe said, "Sondra, don't worry. *And don't touch me whatever you do!*"

Another time I went to the management and complained that I was tired and needed a dressing room that wasn't so far from the stage. The manager of the theatre smiled mischievously and said, "Well, Sondra—we have just the dressing room for you!" It turned out to be Trigger's dressing room. Yes, Trigger from *The Roy Rogers Show*—Roy Rogers' *horse.* It was his stable.

Geoffrey Holder and me, PBS TV

I also did a great deal of summer stock. One show was *Bloomer Girl* with a wonderful actor named Avon Long. His favorite expression was, "For two bits, I'll give you an original piece of business." He was a great dancer, singer, and performer. He was forced to live in another kind of housing in St. Louis, merely because he was black. I learned so much from him.

I met so many wonderful people on the summer road—Howard Keel, Gordon MacRae, Susie Johnson, Paula Stewart—the top musical performers in theatre at that time. I had the chance to do roles that were created before my time—wonderful roles suited for someone my size and for my talent. They were singing and dancing roles. Brilliant book shows with brilliant scores. Summer stock was a fantastic training ground back then, but it was not just for beginners.

Alan Peterson and me, *Street Scene,* NYC Opera

There were twelve thousand people a night at the Muni Opera in St. Louis. And the same with Dallas. It was *big*. They were big!

I did *Angel in a Pawn Shop* in Philadelphia with the great Eddie Dowling. He was the original Tom in *The Glass Menagerie* and at one time had owned the St. James Theatre. His curtain speeches were heartbreaking. He was afraid audiences had forgotten him, which to a degree they had. One night during one of his death-defying curtain call speeches they almost had to use a hook to get him off. He would just come forward and reminisce. His wife, Raye Dooley, who in her day had been a musical comedy star, was now his dresser. Eddie was now an old man. He had trouble remembering his lines. He'd close his eyes to try to see them more clearly. This affected his gestures and I'd be smacked in the head or socked in the eye. The truth is, he really had accomplished all that he said he had done. It was so sad that so few people out there really knew who he was. A sad, sad end to his formidable career.

Angel in a Pawn Shop, Eddie Dowling and me

Yet it's a cruel business. And little by little it begins to hit you that it is and always *was* a business. But for myself, I feel I've been blessed. I was blessed to meet people like Eddie Dowling and I am still blessed with all the new people I meet. It never stops. It's wonderful.

I've never wanted to meet somebody that I haven't really at some point met. There I was. There they were. It happens. However, so much of it is luck. It's your own stuff—your life force, your destiny, but believe it— the more knowledge you have, the more patient and humble you become.

There were periods of unemployment and desperation but there was always something that interested me, whether it was making a good salad or learning a language or reading a new book. I was never just focused on 'one thing.' So many become focused on the short-run. It happens to a lot of people; I see it all the time. "I want it now. I want them to see me now. I have to have it now." This is infantile behavior. Even if you never received the support of your family, it's still infantile.

My own mother never knew if she was supportive towards me or competitive. Perhaps she was a frustrated theatre-performer. Children often have opportunities that their parents wanted for themselves. I feel that if you have a gift, it beckons you to do specific things. I think the gift begins clamoring for attention and nourishment. As a kid you begin tap-dancing. Not just because of the need for attention—you can't help it! There are two types of performers—the ones that must have the attention and the ones that can't help it. They just have to do it. They can't do anything else.

The Beginnings

YOU START AT THE BEGINNING. Where the hell is the beginning? It seems to me that I'm starting my fifth or sixth life.

But many beginnings start out with parents. What can I tell you about my parents? We lived in Newark, New Jersey. Family name, Gash. My parents, little brother, and me.

My father's name was David. He was very, very fair, with pale nervous (they quivered) blue eyes. He was one-quarter albino.

(Or so my little brother Saul and I were told.) Dad had light golden blond hair that turned white overnight with such swiftness that I found it awesome.

He came from a comfortable family. The women were well educated; the men were not. They worked in a successful family business supplying syrups and carbonated water for bars and candy stores. Yet my father sort of disowned himself, since he was perceived by his family as the 'bad kid.' He was often disciplined severely. As a teenager he woke up one morning with a tattoo on his lower right arm, which was the result of a night of drinking. He was ashamed of it; he kept it covered most

Mom & Dad on their honeymoon

Saul & me

of the time for his whole life. Today his tattoo would have been a smash, but judged these days to be not too creative—an anchor and the initials U.S.A.

My mother's name was Belle, maiden name, Rosenfeld. (I have often thought it should have been Belle Out of Order! If you catch my drift, she was a walking time bomb.) Belle, Mom, was as dark as my dad was fair. Black eyes, olive skin, more gypsy. She could be out in the sun for hours. When my father went anywhere near the sun, he would burn terribly. His blue-white skin would almost peel off in ribbons. I do not ever recall either acknowledging or celebrating any of our birthdays.

I spent much of my childhood being sickly. I had pneumonia on a regular basis. I was also given growth hormone injections because my family was alarmed that I was so tiny. I looked forward to all of this even though I had no idea what it was about. However, after I would get the injections, we'd go to the movies and then have Chinese food.

It seems to me that I'm the living proof that growth hormones did nothing for me. I mean nothing. A sheer disaster. I am still just under five feet tall—four feet ten and one half inches.

I did have one teacher who was sensitive to how I felt about being so short. In her class when we would line up in order of our size, she would have me stand in second place. Yes, she was terrific.

What can I tell you about public school? Not much.

I wandered through those gray halls of education. My mind and body were simply somewhere else. I was only happy when the teacher was out and we were lucky enough to have to wait for the substitute teacher. I'd become quite animated and cheerfully looked forward to entertaining my classmates with a little song, dance or recitation—even from the beginning.

My parents did not appear to be all that interested in me or what I did or even in each other. However, there I'd be in the same chair at the same time each night for dinner—with all of my fantasies.

I had a pal named Mrs. Magenty. She was an old woman who lived in the house next to ours. She liked me enough to let me dance on her parquet floor and ride the arms of her sofa like a horse until one of them broke off. One day she smiled really wide and scared me to death—she didn't have *one* tooth in her mouth. She wanted me to stop crying, so she showed me her teeth in a glass filled with water. One time I stole flowers from the cemetery near our house just for Mrs. Magenty. I sang for her birthday from the top of her garage roof and tried to hit a high note the way a 'star' would, and fell off the roof to the ground. When she held me in her arms, I told her, "I've seen God, and He looks just like you."

And then a few days later, she suddenly died.

I could delight her no more.

But now I was dancing on other floors.

I entered the world of tutus and glitter. I had received a scholarship at a local dancing school to study with Miss Hortense Greenwald.

Each season, as a very young child, I appeared in her recitals.

I can remember a few in particular. I still see myself wearing a blue stiffly starched tarlatan tutu with rosebuds and point shoes with silver paint as I danced to the music of Léo Delibes. I can still see the fancy lettering on the sheet music. In another recital, I danced the *Spider Dance* wearing a black tutu with silver sprinkles on the top layer of the skirt and the same silver painted point shoes but 'freshened up a bit.' I also danced to *Waltz of the Flowers*.

Me in tutu with rosebuds

And then I waltzed right into the YMHA Players.

I was 10 or 11 years old when I first met Mr. George Kahn. He ran the YMHA Players, which was a wonderful community theatre in Newark, New Jersey. To me he was Santa Claus. He was a portly gentleman with white curly hair who chomped on cigars and wore a vest. He was quite encouraging and invited me to perform for a real audience. And I did. I had only just begun high school.

And then—I waltzed right to the Catskills.

The Catskills, or
Mrs. Ader's Walnut House on the Hill

One of the members of the YMHA Players was Sam Seidler, a grade school teacher. During the summers in the Catskill Mountains he was social director of a hotel called Mrs. Ader's Walnut House on the Hill. Yes, this truly was the name. I'm not making it up.

Sam was a slight, sweet man with a rather aquiline nose and a pencil-thin mustache. He wore a toupée and he thought no one was aware of it. If he hadn't been so dear and gentle he might have been mistaken for a pimp. The only thing that saved him was the fact that he wore thick glasses and had a faint speech impediment. He invited me to the Catskills to perform in a variety show he was directing called the *Hi Neighbor Revue*.

Hi Neighbor Revue, Sam Seidler, Fritzie Burr, and me

The Catskills were a great training ground for performers. On weekends the comics would entertain, rotating from hotel to hotel. I learned so much from knowing them and watching them. I listened and I learned. Their timing was fantastic and, needless to say, they were hilarious. Buddy Hackett, Jack Carter, Julie Oceans, Joey Adams, and Red Buttons were just a few who I met. To this day I still fall down laughing at almost anything I hear them say; of course, most of it is on recordings or roasts from old TV programs.

One afternoon in the Catskills, Buddy Hackett was playing baseball. Someone whacked the ball way, way out there. He jumped into his car leaving a trail of dust just to fetch it! He screeched back to the field and threw the ball to home plate. Funny? Or insane? Funny!

I performed in the *Hi Neighbor Revue* for almost an entire summer. Not only was it the name of our revue, it was also the name of our opening song, which was long and extended. The entire cast (four of us) would walk through the audience shaking hands with them, and sing while they were listening to a bugle call, which was coming from the piano.

> *Hi Neighbor! Hi Neighbor!*
> *What do you know and what do you say?*
> *We'll chase your worries away.*

It went on like that until we reached the platform. Then we lined up facing the audience; they were applauding and throwing us grateful kisses although we hadn't even done anything on stage yet!

Sometimes there would be a piano, drums, saxophone, and maybe a clarinet. The musicians consisted of the same waiters who were also frantically cleaning tables. If they were off-duty, we'd have more musicians. I had very few costumes, even though as a young dancer my suitcase was already stuffed with ribbons, safety pins, and peroxide to keep my hair blonde (blonde like my Dad's), a color I was so enchanted with. I'd dab my hair with cotton swabs, which left a faint medicinal odor that never quite rinsed off.

What can I tell you about the dances I performed at this time?

They came from my imagination. I would wait in the wings during these revues, watching the other variety acts with great passion, hoping to give my all to 'say something significant.'

The poems and skits were mostly in Yiddish (the YMHA was the Young Men's Hebrew Association, after all). I'd tremble with reverence as Fritzie Burr recited *The Ballad of the Harp Weaver* by Edna St. Vincent Millay. I was so moved that I'd mouth the words along with her. She was an amazing woman (later playing Fanny Brice's mother in *Funny Girl*) who was a comedian, poetry reader, and—in her estimation—a femme fatale. To me, she resembled Olive Oyl, Popeye's girlfriend.

Fritzie decided I needed to be tutored about sex. She tried with great kindness to teach me how to be a good kisser. She instructed me by using an orange. "When your lips go like this, it means this. If it goes like that, it means this. Then sometimes there could be a tongue!" It was turning out to be a terrific summer. I loved the beauty of poetry and song and Fritzie was an expert in delivering both.

There was another song in the revue I distinctly remember called, "I Went Down to the Saint James Infirmary." It was alluring and plaintive. I was consumed with the desire to interpret this sorrowful song through dance. I wanted to dance my feelings and tell the story, the drama.

And I did.

My set was a simple table. I wore a black leotard, black elastic diamond-shaped tights with seams up the back, and high-heeled shoes. On my head was a derby hat with a feather I added from my valise.

Why a hat?

Why a feather?

I haven't the faintest idea. Drama, I suppose. The lyrics were so sad. This was something I just had to do.

Every bit of intensity went into my movements. They could be bluesy, funky, grieving, or anything. I'd end with a slow, slow cartwheel and a split that would leave my legs spread-eagle on top of a table. At this conclusion, the six 100 watt bulbs were dramatically lowered to black out!

There was a gasp from the audience, then silence. I was sure the audience was awestruck. This was followed by some applause and then, a little more applause, and then...lots of yelling.

It was Mrs. Ader. She was screaming that I was fired. "How *dare* you do that dirty dancing on my stage! My hotel!"

I was promptly replaced by Eleanor Trieber, a dancer from New York City, who years later would be my understudy in *High Button Shoes*! Fortunately I had already performed most of the season of the *Hi Neighbor Revue* before the disgrace of my dismissal.

Our accomodations at the hotel were shabby screened-in cabins on the grounds. We had metal cots and a small chest of drawers. The bathrooms were wooden outhouses not far from our quarters with a makeshift outside shower. We were permitted to eat our meals in the dining room with the other guests.

On weeknights, the guests were women with children. Their husbands were still in the city working and only arrived on weekends. The women played cards, bingo, and received dancing lessons and often flirted with busboys, waiters, social directors—any available male.

Yes, it was an incredible place until my erotic dance to the plaintive "Saint James Infirmary." I quickly recovered.

Madame Alexandra Danilova and other Teachers

I MUST HAVE BEEN SEVEN OR EIGHT the first time I saw a play. It was in Newark, New Jersey at the Mosque Theatre. I considered the Mosque to be the mecca of culture.

It was there I saw the touring company of *Peter Pan*.

Oh, the magic of that play! Peter Pan flew from a rope that was thick enough to have pulled up the *Andrea Doria*, but I still believed it all. Every bit of it. "I am youth! I am joy! I am FREEEEDOOOOOM!" I screamed. "Peter, take me with you!"

The trips to the mecca of culture weren't that frequent. My mother rarely took me; instead, it was more often my Aunt Dinah, the teacher, who took me. It didn't matter if we were sitting in the last row.

When she took me to see the *Ballet Russes de Monte Carlo*, my life changed forever. I was staggered after seeing the great Madame Alexandra Danilova dance. I have no idea how I found the gumption to find the stage door and go backstage, but I did. I don't even remember if my Aunt Dinah took me. I was probably only ten years old at the time. But suddenly before me was the great Danilova.

I have vivid memories of her. I remember my eyes zooming in to take in her full image. She was sitting on a squat trunk filled with pink satin point shoes. Her gorgeous legs were long, lean, and crossed in a pin-up style. She wore high-heels and had a perfect marcelled hair-do. Her whole body seemed to be resting effortlessly on one hip. What amazing balance. It seemed as though she had been lifted that way by the arms of a strong partner. Delicately, between her fingers, she was folding back the silver foil of a Hershey Bar. Her lipstick was bright red and her mouth glamorous like the red wax lips we bought as children in candy stores.

I somehow got her address. I wrote her a long, tear-stained letter about my need to dance. I mentioned that I was the best in the local dancing school but I was sure that I hadn't had the proper amount of training. Whatever I said, it must have struck a note with her because I received a personal response from Madame Alexandra Danilova, Ballerina Absoluta, from the Park Vendome Apartments in New York City.

She invited me to come and dance for her.

On a given afternoon, I put together an outfit I thought was a knockout—a navy blue and white polka-dot pleated roller skating skirt; a light-blue palm tree blouse, which buttoned down the front; clean, white cotton underwear fresh from the clothes line; and a pair of Eurythmics slippers used for acrobatics. I took off for New York City and the rehearsal studio of the *Ballets Russes de Monte Carlo*, located somewhere in mid-town.

Madame Danilova cleared the room at lunchtime. There was a pianist. "*Dence* for me," she said with her head gesturing invitingly. I followed her command with a vengeance. When some time passed and the dust had cleared, she suggested I jump in the air and turn. I obliged. She smiled. "Now *tvice* in the air *vid* turn." I obliged. "Now tree dimes!" I tried.

And fell.

I'm sure this creature flying wantonly through space must have been hilarious to Madame Danilova. I remember how solemn and respectful she appeared to be. Yet I was sent in haste to the Swoboda School that very day and I was given a scholarship.

On the train home to Newark, I was delirious with joy. As it chugged through Secaucus and Hoboken (you could smell Secaucus) everything was just perfect. It all crashed when I got home. My mother decided that this was charity on Madame Danilova's part. I was just a pint-sized kid who had no future in the fancy arts. "Highfalutin' ideas! No, you can't accept; they'll laugh at you, you dummy," she said.

> **SWOBODA SCHOOL of BALLET**
> MARIA YURIEVA — VECHESLAV SWOBODA
>
> Dear Sondra: —
> Because you were sent to us by the "Ballet Russe", we feel a special interest in your work. We should appreciate your sending us a note telling us of your plans.
> Best wishes to you and your Mother!
>
> 50 WEST 57th STREET • NEW YORK • COlumbus 5-9857

re: Madame Danilova

I was still in grammar school and wasn't enjoying school at all. There was only one teacher named Mrs. Johnson who was aware of me and the fact that I was gifted. It made perfect sense that she was an art teacher! I just couldn't wait to get out of school, and I did at a young age. Later, the only other teacher I liked in high school was the truant officer, Mr. Freedman. He certainly knew I was never going to be a product of the educational system. I had a tendency to walk in the front door in the morning and say, "Good morning, Mr. Freedman" and then walk out of the door while whispering to myself, "Good day, Mr. Freedman." He knew I wasn't a bad kid; but he knew I was the one who would walk in the front door and walk out the back door. Years later he would come to see me backstage in *High Button Shoes*. But that's later.

After my mother said I couldn't accept the scholarship, I wrote to Madame Danilova again. My chutzpah must have been award-winning. This time I was sent with her blessings to Studio 61 at Carnegie Hall. Virginia Lee, a plump, bossy woman feared by all, was the administrator of the school. And once again, I was accepted in New York City.

What a thrill it was to go up in the old wooden elevator at Carnegie Hall and hear the music from the piano as you approached. You knew it was a special place. This time I arrived with a better version of what I thought classical ballet attire should be. I found royal blue tights for skiers with zigzag ribbing—a most fetching design—on sale in a local department store in

Newark. I wore a little cotton top with rabbits on it. I was sent to the barre at the far end of the room and stood between two male dancers—Grant Moradoff and André Eglevsky. Thank God I was naïve enough not to know who these guys were for they were already quite famous in the dance world. I tried to copy what they did. I hadn't yet realized I'd been placed in the professional class because of Madame Danilova's recommendation.

Then came *grande battements*—those big, controlled kicks—front first, then back. The combination 8-8-4-4-2-2-1-1 followed by eight swings to and fro. All hell broke loose.

I kicked the shit out of both of them. I was unfamiliar with the combination—the counts were in Russian and French. I gave it everything I had. They didn't *want* everything I had!

So I began to study a new technique. This is part of a dancer's life. We are nomadic and study different techniques all the time. And different teachers.

Vera Nemchinova, a Russian teacher I studied with for a while at *Studio 61*, was a bit of a 'nipper.' As she called combinations, she would stare a great deal at herself adoringly in the mirror, but she was still a wonderful teacher. Then there was Madame Anderson, who had her own school and sprinkled you with a watering can, as well as the floor, if she wasn't crazy about your work.

And then there was my greatest teacher, Eddie Caton, who was truly unique and inspiring. Eddie would ask people to take a look at me. He wore a sailor hat all the time. I was in my secret hiding place, under the piano, when word came that Eddie's mother had just died. He sat at the piano and played "Saint James Infirmary." *"Saint James Infirmary."* I felt so mysteriously connected to him. Then came Olga Tarassova, a dark Russian beauty … but more about her later.

I had made only one good friend during my early days of studying dance in New York. Her name was Viola. She was originally from Connecticut but had already rented a tiny room by herself in New York City. I was in the early days of high school and living at home in New Jersey, but as often as I could, I would spend the night. Viola was from Syrian or Lebanese descent. She was quite large, which was atypical for a dancer. She had a large head, a sturdy body, and was slightly overweight. She had large square teeth and large, black, innocent eyes. Yes, everything about Viola was large. Yet her love for dance was burning, as incandescent as mine. In her tiny room was a hot plate with a single burner. We would make oatmeal on that burner, boil an egg, and then use the same water from the boiled egg to make cocoa. This was our breakfast before class in the morning.

Although Viola had a large, round body and I had a tiny, round body, both of us were still getting rid of baby fat. But the baby fat had to go; as dancers, we had to be longer and leaner.

There was a man who made rubber tights, which would make you sweat, that we wore under our woolen ones. The rubber was thick and closed at the seams and it was the color of piggy pink. It made farting sounds when you danced—it sounded like a whoopee cushion. Pools of sweat would dribble down your legs on to the floor and then you might slip and fall right into it. Not a pretty picture, but a great deal about dance is falling down. And it *was* a way to get rid of that baby fat!

The dream of a dancer never ends. Every class begins with a ritual. And how I loved that ritual.

Oh, the joy of those little changing rooms! Butts in the air, turned-out feet. Delicate pink bodies bent in reverence over their tights. Cupping lambs wool over their toes, then carefully sliding their feet into point shoes. The barre, the discipline—all minds set to hear the teacher and the music. And the warmth spreading over your body with the muscles and joints responding—oh my. There is nothing as sweet. Extensions pulling, stretching. The arms holding mirages of bouquets of flowers. The blue veins beginning to appear from effort on the forehead—popping out like cords on your arms.

Dancers are obsessed with their craft. They must dance, train, and rehearse. A dancer is unique. We regard ourselves like a piece of sculpture, or a machine, or a puzzle. The dancer stares at his or her figure in the mirror. Yet, while doing so, there is not an ounce of vanity. The look is about movement and not the person. It's about the character through the eyes of the choreographer seen through movement. It's not about ego. Such gorgeous, hard work.

A typical morning in the life of a dancer. This is how all mornings begin. And this ritual is as necessary as drinking water. It is the closest to a religion that I have ever known.

Bando, Bindo, or Marlon Brando

I was given a scholarship to study with Olga Tarassova. She taught a clear technique. She was also one of the only teachers who offered soothing affection, which was sorely needed by sensitive students. And boy, did I need it.

There was a haughty dancer in one of her classes who was quite mean to me. Elena was a good dancer and behaved like the teacher's pet—which she was. I was extremely envious and sensitive to her slightest sneer. Her family had people "in the business." She always made me feel keenly aware of being poor. After class, we'd all go down the street on 57th to Horn and Hardart's Automat. But Elena never invited me to join her and her group—not once. Petty things like this were common.

One day, a handsome young fellow came to see Elena. He sat quietly and watched us dance. When class was over he smiled at me. I rushed off quickly so he wouldn't see me blushing. I was thrilled because I knew I had danced well. Then I saw the snooty Elena Karina leave with this young, handsome fellow. I disliked Elena. Yes, I was jealous of her but he had smiled at *me*. Viola, my only friend in class, said his name was Bindo or Bambo—Marlon *Brandin*, or something like that.

This was the first time I saw Marlon Brando.

One day after class Madame Tarassova introduced me to a Mr. Besoff. He owned a restaurant called The Russian Tea Room on 57th Street. He had a similar restaurant club in Washington, D.C. He offered me a job to perform in sketches in the Russian language. It sounded just like the Catskills, but spiffier. I accepted on the spot. Even though I was under age, no one asked. I still lie about my age to this day.

The Balalaika in Washington, D.C. turned out to be just like the *Hi Neighbor Revue*, except in Russian. There were better costumes and scenery and the revue featured an extra attraction of a sword swallower who reeked of vodka. Only when he was sober was he a darling. The cast was comprised of two older Russian couples who sang in Boyar costumes and performed Mrs. Ader-like skits. They were kind and patient with me. And now I had new Russian expressions, like '*ou ou ou maylaiyou, ach, ach*' to add to my Yiddish expressions, such as '*ich bach badder in draid.*'

I danced spirited Russian dances wearing bright green high boots, embroidered blouses, and brightly colored flowered skirts. On my head I wore a wreath of flowers with long streaming colored ribbons attached to it. I danced, combining both the male and female parts. Sometimes my partner was the sword swallower who smelled of kerosene when not drinking vodka. One evening, I danced to "Waltz of the Flowers" in a quickly rented, not-so-white tutu, since Mr. Besoff promised me I could do serious ballet while I was in this revue. Now, my new name was Shura Sondra.

One night, a famous painter came to see the show and wanted to paint me. I asked everyone in sight, "Should I?" The answer was "He's famous; you'll be famous." How flattering. So I went to his hotel. I wore my little grey-blue practice leotard. The famous bearded painter mixed his paints. At first he arranged me like a 'still life' seated in a chair—and then lying on a bed. He told me to 'move this way and then that way.'

The famous (painter) told me of the famous book he had written about Tibet.

"Wow," I said.

"In Tibet," he said, "I have learned about massage with talcum powder."

"Wow," I said again.

I got it.

Just in time to run, grab the phone, and lock myself in the bathroom. Mercifully, I remembered the orchestra leader's number. I bolted out of the bathroom, rushing past the famous painter, who must have been stunned with my swiftness and his slowness after all those years studying 'talc' in Tibet. I ran in my little leotard, and took the elevator to the lobby of the famous painter's hotel. I was saved by the bandleader, who at that moment had just arrived in his car—like Superman—to save me. As he raced to me I saw his pajamas underneath his overcoat. He had been asleep when I phoned him. I began to scream and flail about—blubbering and blubbering all about Tibet and talcum powder. I sounded like Mrs. Ader, who used to scream at us in the Catskills.

After that experience, I kept to myself. I was clearly disoriented. I was lonely and embarrassed about not being able to use good old Fritzie Burr's expertise or my own good sense.

Then everything seemed to change.

One morning at breakfast as I read the paper, I came across an advertisement for *The Eagle Has Two Heads*, a play by Jean Cocteau that was coming to Washington, D.C. There was a picture of the two stars, Tallulah Bankhead and Marlon Brando. "I've met him," I thought. He was the handsome actor who had come to class. "That's his name, Marlon Brando," I burst out saying. "I must find him, I have a long lost friend in Washington, D.C!"

The next day I dressed carefully to look like a serious dancer. My hair was pulled back in a ponytail and I wore little ballet slippers. I headed for the Willard Hotel, which was near the National Theatre where the play was to open. When they asked for my name at the desk, I responded that it was "S." I explained that I was in Madame Tarassova's class and a good friend of Elena Karina's.

I knocked on the given door and was met by another young man who said Mr. Brando was in the bathroom and to go right in. After a startling moment of bug eyes from me, I followed his instruction and found Marlon there sitting on the rim of the bathtub with a circle of drums around him, practicing.

He remembered me and hopped right off the tub and formally bowed. I explained what I was doing in D.C., weeping all over his extended hand.

Marlon said he would meet me after my show; we'd sightsee late at night. And we did. More than once we climbed up a statue and placed a container of coffee and a donut in some pilgrim's hand. He was gentle, funny, and honest with me. He never made a pass. I considered him my first real male comrade. He was protective and observant. His concentration never wandered. This was his gift. When you were together, he could make you feel like no one was more important than you.

He told me about the play and his misery of working with Tallulah. I think he wouldn't sleep with her, although he never said so. When I came to his theatre, he never introduced us. He always wore some part of his costume on the street. He taught me how to make a nifty wound with red gels, as he was shot in the play by her character. When I saw the production, I thought he was just okay in it. I felt he just walked through it. He wasn't very happy and he was either dismissed or fired. An actor named Helmut Dantine replaced him.

After that, Marlon wrote to me that we should try to see one another again back in New York. I told him I wanted to live there. He promised to help me convince my folks. In fact, he called them immediately and charmed my mother so completely that she coyly capitulated and said 'yes' if only he promised to look after me.

HOTEL STATLER BOSTON

Dear Sondra,

I've missed you here in Boston.
When are you going home to N.Y.?
You missed me a lot too and I know
your thoughts as you lie in bed just before
you go to sleep. What do you know about that piglet!
Do you ever get the scoffus or the henious anymore?
You are a good girl you know and a smart little yiddle.
The most character revealing incident was when you asked that woman to get your shoes and she wouldn't. It is four o'clock in the morning, and I am completely senseless.
May I sleep with you sometime?

Affectionately,
MARLON

Before Marlon, before Madame Danilova—beginning in childhood—I had always had an enormous need to leave home. As a little girl, I ran away all the time with Dixie, my slightly older friend who was a gypsy. Back at that time when I was living on Elizabeth Avenue in New Jersey, gypsies lived in the area.

Gypsies believe that anything they get their hands on is rightfully theirs, and Dixie would walk away with my underwear and my bobby

Bando, Bindo, or Marlon Brando

To meeting in NY. In memory of the time you wouldn't. — Marlon

pins. It could be anything. And like me, she liked to travel. We believed that if a character boarded a plane or a train when they got off they were exactly where they intended to be, just like in the movies. So one day when we were nine or ten years old, we got in a boxcar on a train. It moved. We moved with it. It stopped and we got off with it. I believe the cops found us in Asbury Park. N.J. They asked us where we were going.

"We're going to see Greta Garbo," we replied.

They thought that was swell, but that our mothers were looking for us. So they put us on the train back home and when we got off we still couldn't understand why Greta Garbo wasn't there.

HOTEL STATLER BOSTON

Dear Sondra,

My recent note was a preposterous distortion of sensitivity. I have no excuse to offer except in the way of an explanation of the peculiar mood I was in, to wit, nutty. Oh Balls! You may as well view me in my purple light as well as my light.

I'm leaving the show "the egal egellelgllge Egale"(can't spell a damm word) Now has only one head. Now that I've left I regret not being able to say goodbye to my FOUL friend because I failed to find any appreciable distiction of the head from the tail and I didn't want to chance being embarassed by addressing the wrong end. I'm especially overjoyed by the fact that my friend Mrs. Egale must lay her eggs without the able assistence of my midwifery. (no soft feelings, of course.)

I would like to see you in N.Y. and carry on with my entrenched Obscurities of purposes and action.

Goodnight, Double Ugly!

MARLON

Ne M'oublier pas ce soir
Tonight, in your bed, put me in your mind, in your heart, and in your body. For only by completeness can one obtain happiness.

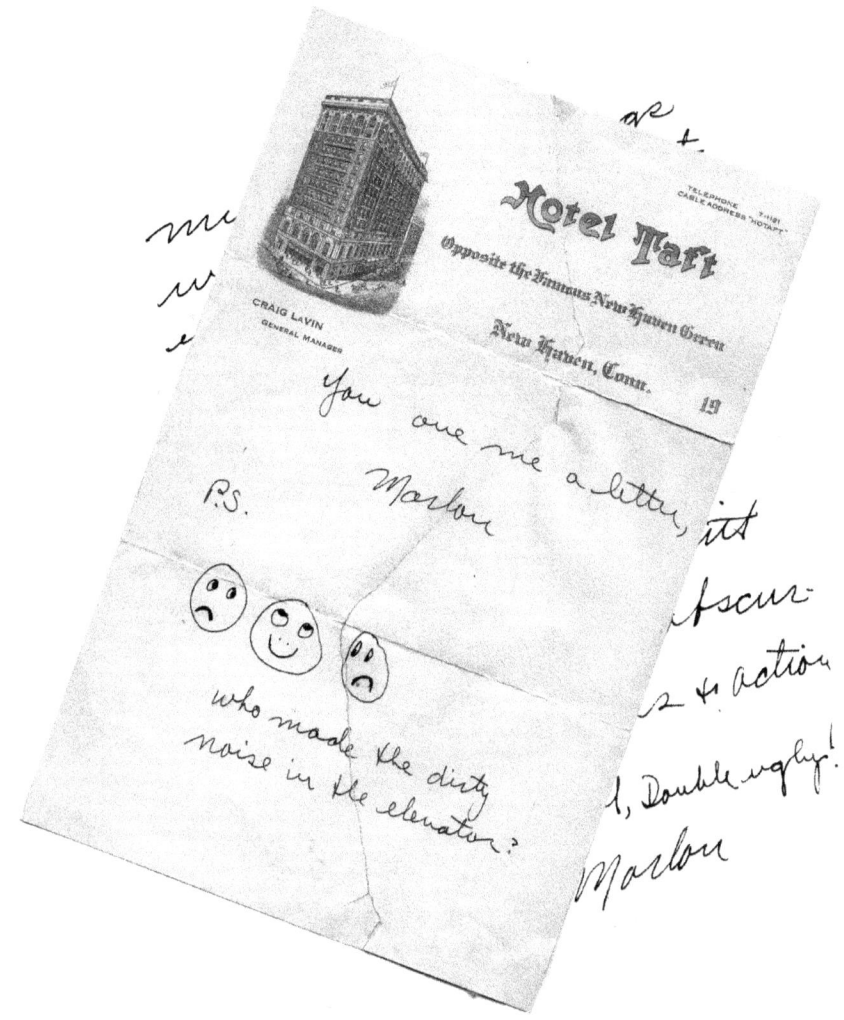

Yes, I ran away my whole life. A regular run-away-er. I used to pack my socks in tissue paper and hide with them in the basement, not knowing where I wanted to go, but knowing I had to go. And now for the first time I truly was going. My little suitcase was packed.

I can still remember my mother lying in bed and the crack of the apple she was eating when I said goodbye. I was frightened, but I was also excited. My father slipped me ten bucks and I never turned back. There was nothing to go back for. I never went home again.

My new life in New York was about to begin.

And Marlon did not disappear.

Marlon, Others, and the Park Savoy

MY FIRST APARTMENT WAS AT THE PARK SAVOY. *What am I saying?* It was a room in a boarding house, located between 6th and 7th Avenues on 58th Street. Marlon had arranged for me to share a room with Florence. I never knew her last name but she was the girlfriend of a close friend of Marlon's named Darren Dublin. Darren, a very witty guy with big teeth, was an actor who eventually became the head of the Actors Extras Union in Los Angeles.

The walls at the Park Savoy were a drab, bluish green beneath years of filth. Each floor was made up of a cluster of wings. Each wing had several rooms and a communal kitchen with a cabinet, some shelves, a refrigerator, and a sink. I don't remember cooking anything in that kitchen, but I do remember a woman from a nearby room humming as she dyed her stockings black because her husband had just died.

There is one particular memory I have of Florence. Her cat. She named him Pastrami because she found him at a delicatessen. Pastrami would fly across the room and spring at the wall, twist his neck, and stare menacingly at me as he slid down.

I thought Florence was pretty sophisticated. She used to cut the tops of her sweaters off in a circular dip and stitch them, which I thought was very beguiling. She wore little pearl earrings and had beautiful light auburn hair with delicate, fair shell-pink skin that redheads often have. When she spoke, her voice was light and had a slight nasal sound that was almost apologetic. She also was, without a doubt, certifiably cuckoo. I was undone most of the time in that tiny room.

Marlon had a room several floors below. Only later did I realize that his mistress, Celia Webb, was also ensconced on his floor in another wing. I didn't even know what a mistress was. Celia was an older Colombian woman. She had a little boy—not his—whom I never saw. It was like out of a novel to me, living at the Park Savoy. Each time I saw Celia, she was in pale pink satin peignoir. Her build was delicate, her hair long and black and knotted in a bun at the nape of her neck. She spoke from the side of her mouth.

I'd knock on Marlon's door frequently just to ask an innocent question. His room was quite small; one narrow window faced the street. There was a small, single bed that always had a head of hair—not his—peeking out of the top sheet. Usually he would say rather sweetly that he would speak to me later. Once he said, "This is Ellen." But all I saw was two slits of dark eyes.

The truth is I never gave the head of hair under the sheets much thought. It wasn't about privacy or territory. I suppose it was about sex but I wasn't quite 'there' yet. On a small table at the side of Marlon's bed was a picture of a beautiful, blond woman. I was told by his friend Darren that her name was Blossom Plum—a great love of Marlon's. But I never met her.

If I wandered about in a bit of a daze, it's not hard to understand why. There was so much coming and going. People, friends and strangers, were dropping in all the time and sitting and watching and leaving. I'm not sure who many of them were. I never had a clue.

I felt like I was Alice in Wonderland. Often I have felt that my life has been a series of rooms that I ventured into, lingering and leaving. I'd half register what I saw and made no judgments. It was not from professional or social ambition or even fickleness—it was simply from an overwhelming curiosity. Or perhaps an insecurity about things I had not yet seen, learned, or been subjected to. Right now I was learning about Marlon and his life and trying not to make any judgments. But I did pay attention.

Marlon had many friends that seemed to me very savvy—Maureen Stapleton, Janice Mars, and Billy Redfield—to name a few.

One of Marlon's closest friends was Wally Cox. I knew him long before he became a comedian, long before his monologues that led him to engagements at The Blue Angel and on to Broadway and then eventually to *Mr. Peepers* fame. At the time, Wally was a talented craftsman who made wonderful jewelry. Once he made me a daisy from a penny to cheer me up on a gloomy afternoon. In those days, he would constantly announce to everyone that he had crabs, but always in a gentle, soft-spoken voice, which was one of his signatures. Although he laughed a great deal, his was never a guffaw but rather a quiet, muffled, cackling sound. He had a small frame but hands and arms of enormous strength. His skin was the color of a baby's skin—smooth and pink. And he was rarely without glasses, wearing big, plastic no-color frames.

Bud (his nickname) and Wally acting silly

Wally told me years later that it was a good thing he became a celebrity because sometimes when he was just standing on the platform waiting for a subway, he was picked up by the police because he resembled every pervert, thief, and demented person in their files. Needless to say, his family history was a mess.

His mother was a horrid, embarrassing drunk. He remained close with his sister and when their mother died, he told me they had a picnic at her grave. They were relieved she had passed out of their lives.

I remember Wally's girlfriend, Marilyn Gennaro. She was a very talented dancer who was otherworldly. To my eye, she possessed a savage beauty—white Kabuki skin, black hair, and black eyes that sparkled as she spoke. She had a quiet voice like Wally's. They both sounded as though they were whispering to you. They seemed meant for each other: they eventually did marry and had a daughter named Alice. And once again, I felt like Alice in Wonderland.

Marlon had bizarre friends. One was Sidney Shaw, a very sharp-witted and very gay guy. He wrote a song called "Evil Spelled Backwards Is Live." There was Igor, the crazy violinist who played on the street outside Carnegie Hall. And another man named Rubenstein who wore a grey fedora and never said a word. He would just sit in my room or Marlon's from time to time. Sometime later he and his mother were murdered in his fancy Fifth Avenue townhouse.

Yes, I felt like Alice in Wonderland down the rabbit hole.

The most trustworthy of people who really held Marlon to task were Philip Rhodes, his makeup man and father figure and alter ego, *whatever*, and Philip's wife, Marie, who was Marlon's stand-in. He had them with him always, if he could. They chided him and guided him and most of the time, he listened. They were truly important to Marlon and two of the dearest people on the planet. Philip's knowledge, from a long-ago time (like the Barrymore clan), was rich.

The First Time

THE FIRST TIME MARLON AND I HAD SEX was not in a romantic setting. We were at his friend Darren's apartment, and Darren was still living with his father in the Bronx. His Dad wasn't home and it was late. There were others there but I found myself in a room alone.

Marlon casually breezed through the room.

We were talking and then we weren't.

It wasn't the sexual experience of my dreams with bells, music, and the heavens parting and my deep passions unleashed.

Frankly, it just hurt. I was confused by my first sexual experience and a bit embarrassed that there were others in the apartment. Marlon gently told me that in two months time I would think about "it" again and feel a lot more curious.

Marlon was right. He knew I'd be thinking about "it" again.

And I was.

We made love quite often and well. My body became alive and responsive to what pleased him, and aware of my own desires. No acrobatics or posing, none of that business. Mutual pleasure sounds—he was slow, sensual, aware, and patient. His body was smooth to touch and so it was with mine. He moved like a dancer. Marlon Brando was—and forever would be—an unusual, wonderful lover, even then, when I didn't know what I was doing, or what pleased me. Or him. The shared intimate time, speaking of other things, and then a second time, more intense or sometimes softer. And the humor. God, he told funny stories about himself, and the women who DID pose—not mean, just funny, or endearing. He was easy to be with and he was very aware. Almost a female kind of equal. I was never jealous if he was with other women. His women actually liked one another—so it was then.

Marlon Brando and Tennessee Williams had similar vibes. If you were drawn to them, it was like being caught by a magnet in a minefield. Once you were caught, it was not easy to escape. They could hold you fast. You could observe, listen, play, laugh, make love...but you were held by that seductive magnet. Marlon could call friends, male or female, at any hour of the night to come over—and they would—whether it was to play chess, or listen to him talk, or make love. They would eagerly go.

I would venture to say that he had this power until the end. Even if he appeared in a thick, wool sweater, you could bet that underneath was a soft, sensual shirt as soft and sweet as his skin. His hands were fascinating. They were wrinkled and deeply marked but his touch was still the touch of an angel.

Before our friendship and subsequent affair, I still had never seen him act except for his unenthusiastic role in *The Eagle Has Two Heads*. I didn't know him as Marlon the great, young actor, nor was I aware that there was this great fuss about him. He'd say to me, "When you get to be twenty-four years old, you're going to be a fascinating woman." Well, I couldn't wait. I stared in the mirror hoping to see what he saw. What a promise to look forward to.

Around this time I got a part-time job as a model at the Art Students League on 57th Street. I think I'm the only model in the history of the Art Students League where there is not one sketch, painting, or drawing that was ever completed of me. I would start to pose, facing to the right, and by the time I was finished, I'd be posing the other way, facing left. The first day that I modeled, I fell off the stand. I swooned and collapsed. You first start with 'short' poses. But then they go on for an hour. And you have to stay in the same position, which isn't an easy thing to do. I was a costume model and, of course, I was falling off the stand. But entertaining!

Marlon was a member of the Actors Studio. He took me to see one of their productions: the play was *La Ronde*. It was the first time I saw Bea Arthur, Steve Hill and Peggy Feury. They were wonderful. I told Marlon that I wanted to be a member of the Actors Studio some day. He promised that I could study with his teacher, Stella Adler. He kept his promise and took me to her.

Marlon never was an active member of the Actors Studio but they certainly used his name a great deal. But he did pay homage to Stella

Adler, who was his teacher. And he was helpful to the Actors Studio when asked. However, he was simply there during those days because of Elia Kazan, Tennessee Williams, and Harold Clurman, Stella's husband at the time. As for Lee Strasberg, Marlon never liked him. Ever.

Some time later, after my friendship with Marlon and Wally was well established and they both had found success, Wally purchased land in Rockland County. We would journey there on their motorcycles. Marlon's passion for bikes had already begun. He felt free that way, because cars always avoided motorcycles on the streets and on the highway. We would have small parties up there in Rockland, which included Marilyn, Billy, Wally, Marlon, and me.

What hard work we did. Schlepping rocks to sit on, digging a big hole and filling it with twigs, and building a fire. We often went there in the late fall or early winter. We ate steak pierced on long, pointed sticks followed by marshmallows. Tears would stream down our cheeks and our noses ran like little children's. We were good friends having a peaceful, happy time filled with laughter and tender feelings for one another. We told stories about our families and we shared secrets. Marlon once said that "he drank from the fountain of my affection."

And then late, late at night we would put out the fire and head home. I think about sitting in front of that fire and the beautiful simplicity of it all and how almost all of them are gone—Wally, Marilyn, Billy, Maureen, and Marlon. So many from that time are no longer alive. Yet the fire burns just as bright illuminating these wonderful faces.

After the Show

Overheard in a gay bar:
I'm not a lesbian… I am an American!

* * *

IN THE 1950S, AFTER OUR SHOWS ON BROADWAY were over, we would go to nightclubs such as The Blue Angel, Crosstown East, and Café Society Downtown. They were fantastic, intimate jazz clubs located on 52nd Street. At the Blue Angel I saw Kaye Ballard, Kirkwood and Goodman, Russell Nype, Felicia Saunders, Portia Nelson, and Wally Cox, to name a few. Or you could go downtown to The Village Vanguard run by Max Gordon and see Judy Holliday, Adolph Green and Betty Comden—all before they were famous. Adolph, Betty, and Judy had a wonderful nightclub act called "The Reviewers." It was a combination of topical humor, comedy sketch, and songs. The club was always packed. It was a little before my time, but they became my friends later on.

We often went to gay clubs that put on elaborate productions. My favorite was the 181 Club. The waiters were very butch and appeared in the shows as well. They were *very* serious. Miriam LaValle was a contortionist, an acrobatic dancer extraordinaire, who married one of the waiters who happened to live downstairs from Bud and CeCe Robinson, the ballroom dancing team who were just getting started at the time. Later they opened for Jack Paar or Johnny Carson on tour. The waiters wore tuxedos, ties and tails that fit beautifully, all very serious.

Years before the gifted Dame Edna Everage, there was a drag queen entertainer by the name of T.C. Jones. His face was oval; his eyes were round, dark, expressive, and wondrous. T.C. was bald, had a raspy voice, and on his head wore some black aigrettes (long plumes) that looked like hair. He resembled Bette Davis. He'd often do monologues from her screen tests. This material was *pure theatre*. Today, we have similar artists such as Lypsinka and the gifted actor, writer, everything—Charles Busch.

T.C. left New York to live in San Francisco. He married. Once I visited him when I was playing at the Geary Theatre in some show. There my dedicated artist friend T.C. was working in a store making delicious ice cream. I think he had stopped performing for good. To this day I still have the pale green beaded evening bag he gave me that he wore in one of his shows.

Louis Calhern

Louis Calhern was a huge man who was always elegantly dressed. His gait was slow and grand. He was appearing in *The Play's The Thing* at the Booth Theatre, which was next door to our theater, the Shubert. His nickname for me was "Kimmer" which he told me means "Wench" in Welsh. On Saturday matinees he would fetch me and take me for a stroll around the block. His hands were enormous and graceful. In the play he was in with Faye Emerson, he had an eating scene that was flawless and attention-getting on a grand scale—a real scene-stealer. His chewing, his mouth, his hands, were all fascinating to watch. What a lesson.

I still don't recall how or when the many tours with this elegant Gulliver ever began, nor do I know what those walks were truly about. But, boy, was he spiffy. And there he was with me—Miss Innocent, dumb, dumb "Kimmer." There are few the likes of Mr. Calhern around these days on Broadway.

Lee Grant

It was an afternoon, but not a matinee day. I saw an actress whose name was Lee Grant. There were a series of scenes mounted that day. It might have been at the Shubert Theatre. I was in *High Button Shoes* and very new to Broadway. The scene that she did was from *Moony's Kid Don't Cry*. She bowled me over, just blew me away. The work is still etched into my memory. Lee moved me so deeply that day, and many more times through the years. What a terrific actress she is. And a good director today, as well.

Recently I asked her about that incident. She said, "It had been a 'New Talent' afternoon." Henry Fonda told Sidney Kingsley about her performance, which led to a small role in *The Detective Story* and the beginning of her acting career. And eventually an Academy Award. Maureen Stapleton had a small role in *The Detective Story*, as well. Ya never know, do you?

Ben Hecht

I FIRST MET BEN WHEN I APPEARED in his play *Winkleberg* at the Renata Theatre with Mike Kellen, James Mitchell, and Frances Chaney. It was based on the life of Maxwell Bodenheim, a well-known poet in Greenwich Village who had been a friend of Ben's. Lee Falk, our director, was also known for creating the comic book heroes, *The Phantom* and *Mandrake*.

During *Winkleberg*, I believe Ben and his wife Rose and daughter Jenny rented an apartment on the upper West Side. Later they moved to Nyack, N.Y.

Mike Kellen, James Mitchell, and me

Towards the end of his life Ben was like a "rebel without a cause." He looked like he belonged to another era. He dressed like a snappy, glossy gangster—somber colors, a skinny tie, and flashing eyes. When you got real close, you'd see that the shabby hat turned out to be a *Borsalino* and the jacket was made of vicuña. He was dapper, romantic and had a wonderful sense of humor. Rose was nuts—jealous and dangerous. Jenny, his daughter, would scream out whatever she needed to say. And I'm sure with that family, she knew she wouldn't be heard *unless* she *did* shout at the top of her lungs.

Once I went to visit him after some accident I'd had. "What are you writing about?" I inquired.

"Gidgie."

"Ben, what's that?"

"It's what Polish girls do!" he said.

"Ben, would you read something of mine?" I asked.

"How's your leg?"

"Good," I replied.

"Okay, I'll read it!"

I liked him enormously. He wrote me two beautiful letters, so full of praise. Jenny, his daughter, joined *The Living Theatre*. She died very young while she was still in that company.

Ben Hecht, backstage, *Winkleberg*

Peter Pan

When I was first cast in *Peter Pan* there was much confusion about just what I was going to play. But Jerry Robbins was sure he wanted me in this production; he had something in mind and trusted it to resolve itself, slowly. At this time there was no concept yet of the character of Tiger Lily. So at the beginning of rehearsals I was cast as a potential Lost Boy (and the only female Lost Boy).

The show was scheduled to open in San Francisco at the Curran Theatre (produced by Edward Lester, who owned the San Francisco Light Opera Company), but first we were to rehearse in Los Angeles. I was excited since I'd never been to California. In fact, I'd never been to the west coast. I had recently gotten married to a wonderful actor, Sidney Armus (his nickname was Shimmy), and this would give us the opportunity to travel together.

Frankly, I was oblivious to everything that was happening but I was so anxious to work. Five of us were chosen to go to Los Angeles since a good part of the casting was going to be done there. Bobby Tucker, the assistant choreographer, would be casting the dancers until Jerry arrived in California. Mary Hunter would be the associate director. As soon as the rest of the cast was chosen, we would begin rehearsals. I still remember the Musicians Union Hall with the piano and the shiny hard wood floors that were difficult to dance on. My husband would join me after we opened so we could be together more often. Ours was a young and new marriage, fragile from the beginning. His budding career and mine. The priorities were confusing to us both.

Sidney Armus, my first husband

I traveled alone by train to Los Angeles. It took three days to cross the country. When I arrived, I was whisked away to the ugliest room in some motel off Hollywood and Vine. Just dumped there. That's my memory of arriving in California. With bloodshot eyes, I scanned the space—the bare light bulb hanging from the ceiling in the center of the room—so gray, so sad. That did it. I went ballistic and started wailing. I searched for the phone and called my friend, Movita Castenada, the only person I knew in Los Angeles. She was a beautiful actress and singer who was Marlon Brando's current girlfriend and later to became his second wife. I was wailing and blubbering to her about this place in the middle of nowhere and how I wanted to go home to New York because this certainly wasn't going to be an adventure! I felt she was the right person to talk to. We all loved Movita. She had a full life before she met Marlon. She had been in the original cast of *Mutiny On The Bounty* and was an absolutely gorgeous Mexican woman with black, fiery, glistening eyes. She was like a great stallion in a field —flaring nostrils, lips red as the pulps of cherries. She was worldly, smart, and a great cook who could not only beat Marlon at chess, but she could also put up with his nonsense.

Movita offered to fetch me immediately. Her family was from the Silver Lake district in Los Angeles so she whisked me away to her mother's house where I found myself being quickly introduced to the family—Mamita, Lolita, Pepepitta, Sarita, and last but not least, Jenny. Somehow her sisters believed that I was having an affair with Marlon so they were less than sweet; in fact, they were mean. I was whisked back to the room with the bare light bulb.

Not only was I clueless about my surroundings—I couldn't drive.

I had failed my driver's test in New York. I was never sure if it was because of my diminutive size or whether my sleeve got caught on the steering wheel or because I just couldn't follow the instructions because I was so nervous. Since everyone knew it was necessary that I had my driver's license, with the help of someone's manager...I showed up at some shabby office in the Bronx, staring at a bunch of guys whose noses were bent to one side of their faces as though they had been punched in a boxing ring one too many times. (A friend confided in me that this was "the Mafia.") I leaned forward and whispered to one of them in a confidential way that Pat Pagano had sent me. The man lowered his paper and said in a booming voice, "Why didjah fail dah test, Sondra?" He then accompanied me to the driving test area in his car, along with a gun in the glove compartment.

I failed the test.

The inspector in L.A. made me swear that I could drive so I whistled a happy tune and looked up at the sky with the innocence of Margaret O'Brien, over the rainbow where Judy Garland took us, into the land where Veronica Lake's hair dipped oh so seductively. Then, I parked on the *sidewalk* and passed the test!! A sign that everything would be all right.

Rehearsals began and the character of Tiger Lily evolved. Everyone in Wendy's dream in the original James M. Barrie stage play played two roles, as we do in our own dreams. Nana the dog is the crocodile, Father is Hook. Only Mrs. Darling, the mother, was never a dual role. Barrie stated it was because mothers are the only pure ones. Mary Martin's daughter, Heller Halliday, played Liza and I played Tiger Lily.

Our rehearsal clothes were the inspiration for the Indian costumes. I either wore navy blue pedal pushers or my beloved blue jeans that were patched so many times in an array of different fabrics that there was hardly any denim left. My lovely feather was my own invention. Dorothy Jeakens, our costume designer, allowed me to create Tiger Lily's feather. It was stronger and larger than the others. I loved my vibrant yellow-orange top with turquoise zigzag chevrons that I wore with turquoise pants and sneakers to match.

Mary Martin's costume for Peter went through many changes—the last containing shades of green suede—the variety of fabric like a collage, so subtle. The details were brilliantly done, the patterns of leaves, bits of gold here and there.

Mary's hair was cropped short at the beginning of rehearsals. Her body was lean, trim, and strong. She was enthusiastic from the start and loved Jerry, always taking his direction eagerly. This is at least how I observed it.

As Tiger Lily came to life, so did the Indians. Our dances were based on children's games. They were difficult to sustain: you needed so much energy. All the pounding and jumping—it was all pure dance, but we still looked like children playing. My character, Tiger Lily, was scared to death most of the time and madly in love with Peter Pan, after he saved her in the forest.

My favorite photo

This was the latest version, of which there were zillions!

There were so many changes in Peter Pan that there must have been twenty or more versions of the Indian dance. One night at a preview in

San Francisco, everyone did their own independent version of the dance we thought we were supposed to be doing. It looked like a pinball machine gone wild; utter madness.

Yet, I loved the work. I loved Jerome Robbins. The show had problems but I was oblivious to them. New scenes came in; I'd learn them and then new songs came in and other songs went out.

The team was wonderful. Peter Larkin was the gifted set designer. And there was the wonderful Cyril Richard who played Captain Hook and Peter Foy who designed the secretly rigged flying apparatus. Carolyn Leigh, a bit plump and delicate sounding, wrote the lyrics ("Young at Heart" and "Witchcraft") and gravel-voiced Moose Charlap wrote the music. We were all working hard collaboratively, like a family.

I was given a wonderful song to sing (which did not remain in the show) called "Wild Indians."

> *When on Warpath*
> *We come get you*
> *Beware*

(Today, not politically correct.)

Everyone seemed pleased with me and I was having the time of my life. At some point I moved to 'better digs' but not much better. However, I didn't feel so isolated or alone anymore. I was grateful for the work, the exhaustion and the fun. And then it was on to San Francisco.

I roomed with Kathleen Nolan, who played Wendy, in some hotel that had apartments. Luxury at this point was a sink in a mini-kitchen area. I recall the linoleum on the floor that had a rug motif. We shared a Murphy-type bed. Kathy was young with a beautiful, unique and rich voice. Her hands and fingers appeared fragile, almost boneless. Her hair was a beautiful shade of auburn brown, and she had a very pale, oval-shaped face like the face of a young Irish lass. She also got plotzed a lot and couldn't hold her liquor. Bob Willoughby, who was the main photographer for the show, was smitten with Kathy.

We opened in San Francisco at the Curran Theatre on July 19, 1954. I arrived at the theatre wearing my pink wedgie bedroom slippers. I was so anxious to get there and be the best that I could that I had forgotten to dress up. I received telegrams from people I didn't even

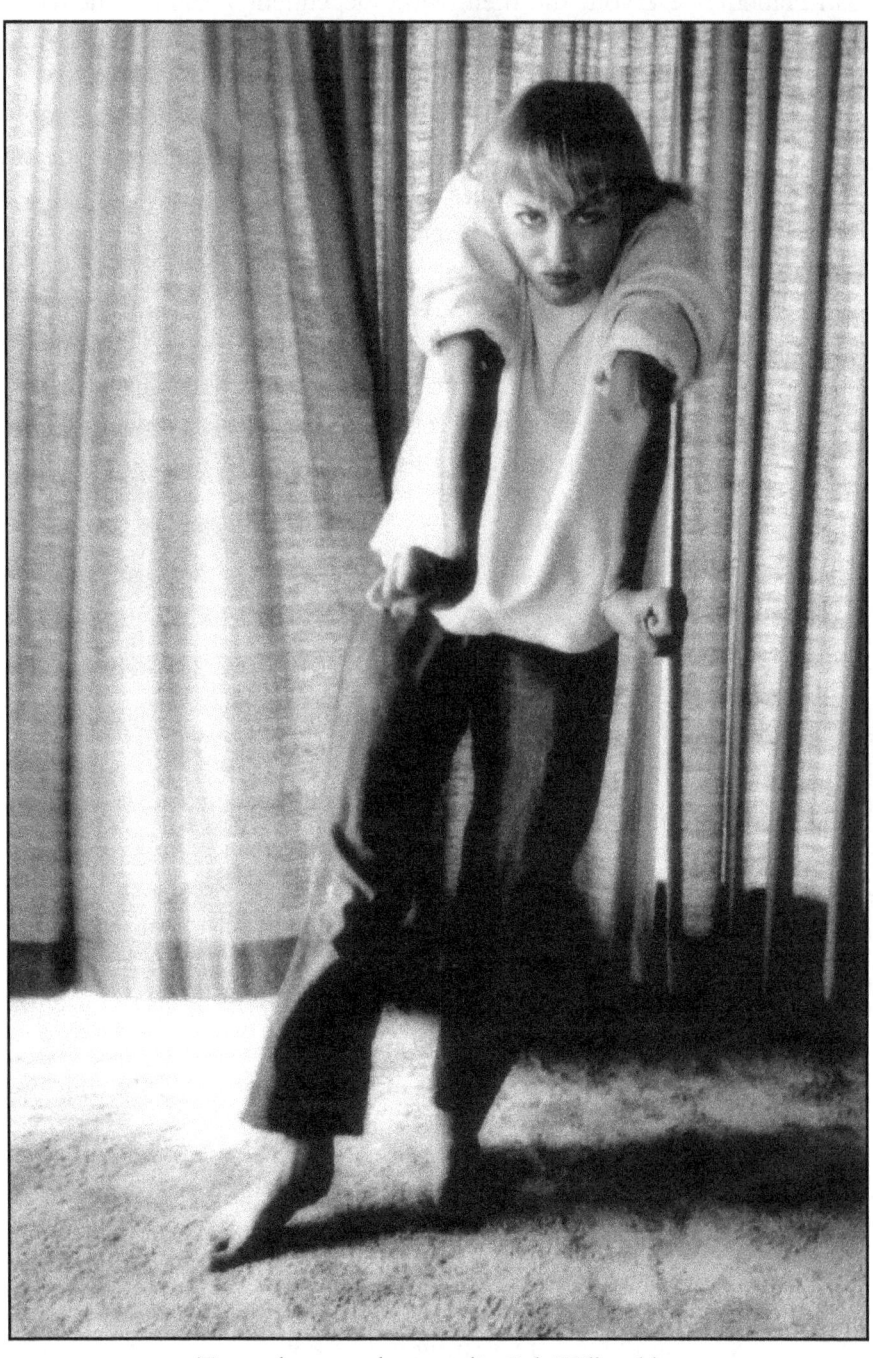

Tiger rehearses; photo credit: Bob Willoughby

Me, Mary, and Yul

know, like Yul Brynner. Apparently, the news was out that I was really good. I was only interested in doing it right.

What I truly never understood is how I became "this year's dessert." I was just simply grateful to play the character of Tiger Lily and was never aware of or understood the politics of show business. When the reviews came out the next day in San Francisco, the critics were gracious. One critic said that Cyril Richard ran away with the show and was 'quickly followed' by Sondra Lee who was 'closely followed' by Mary Martin. Not good! I didn't understand how 'not good' that was. The show was in trouble.

Variety, August 25, 1954

"*Peter Pan* in a musical version, got off to a flying start tonight at the Curran Theatre, San Francisco, thanks to the presence of Mary Martin in the title role and the enthusiasm of the Civic Light Opera company. But whether or not it will be material for New York is debatable. Miss Martin, as Peter, is in one of her best moods, charming, lively, lithe and understanding. Cyril Richard is excellent as the troubled father, and Captain Hook. Sondra Lee is delightful as the whimsical Tiger Lily.

The entertainment lies chiefly in the handling of the ensembles and choruses and the occasional ballets. As a consequence, the point of interest is Captain Hook, rather than Peter Pan, and Miss Martin is in the rather curious position of functioning as a subordinate player, while Mr. Richard emerges as the star of the performance.

In the dance department, Miss Lee has no difficulty establishing herself as an important factor. She has a keen sense of timing and a shrewd method of establishing audience relationships."

Believe me—I had *no* idea what that was supposed to mean! The very next day I arrived at the theatre and was told by Jerry that my song was cut. Here I was so happy and ready to be rewarded for good work. I was devastated. Each day songs were deleted, restaged, substituted. I was learning fast. In the chorus, there was a simply wonderful dancer who played one of the Pirates. He was told that he had to do a backward flip; it was a requirement. This dancer tried and tried and finally he fell and broke his nose. His accident cost him his job! That heartbroken injured dancer was a lad who is now as famous in the dance world as you can get—Mr. Paul Taylor.

One of the songs in the show was very beautiful—the lyrics lean and simple, the melody haunting. It was called "When I Went Home." When that song was cut, I felt compelled to go to Mary and ask her why. She said the song was just too sad and the people didn't applaud. "Mary," I said, "They were taken off guard, they were so moved!" Mary blinked at me with a blank face. "Mary," I said again, "They didn't applaud for the Gettysburg Address either!"

To this day I hope someone records "When I Went Home." The song is what I believe Peter's story is about. (Wendy, playing the 'mother,' puts the little lost boys to sleep. They are arranged in a semi-circle, resting their heads on pillows. So sweet in their sack-cloth shifts. Wendy sits in a rocking chair and asks Peter if he knows a lullaby. He sits by her feet. He is very quiet and then he sings this beautiful song).

When I went Home
I thought that certainly
Someone would leave the door
or window open wide for me.
And surely there would be
A welcome light.
When I went Home
I counted so Upon
Somebody waiting up to ask me questions
On and On
To ask me where I'd gone
Was I alright.
But the door was locked
And the window barred
And I knew with an awful dread
That someone else
Some other boy
Was sleeping in my Bed
When I went home
I found that sad to say
You must expect to be forgotten
Once you've gone away
And so I couldn't stay that lonely night
When I went home.

It must have been around this time when three new figures entered the scene. And the tick, tick, tick of typewriters could be heard in a nearby hotel. Jule Styne, the composer, and Adolph Green and Betty Comden, the lyricists, were on board to help out with the score since the management felt that Carolyn and Moose were too new at this work to be able to work as fast as required. They weren't being replaced—it was just that the family kept growing. They thought the show could be saved.

I still think the songs Moose and Carolyn wrote were responsible for the purity of the true character of the piece. At that time I didn't really know about the behind-scenes happenings. At one point, another song was added—"Ugga-Wug"—and *it* was a song that remained. In the original version Mary Martin (Peter) played the fiddle and Tiger Lily played the frying pan. "Ugga Wug" was a big hit. The response was terrific.

Frank Lindsay, who played a Pirate in Peter Pan came rushing out of his dressing room and shouted to me "Do you believe in fairies?" "Yes, yes!" said I, dashing to the other side of the stage. "Good, thank God—I almost died!" And he returned to putting on his makeup.

* * *

Around that time, Marlon Brando came to see *Peter Pan*. He was in L.A. shooting *Desirée,* the movie about Napoleon. After the show, in the quiet of our dinner he said, "Sondra, why did you push Mary Martin off the stage?" I was dumbstruck by his remark. "I was giving it my all, that's all!" After a few days, "Ugga Wug" became a large production number with the Lost Boys, the Indians—the whole group. No more fiddle, no more frying pan—but it served the show well. Let's face it, when a show revolves around a star, you may be terrific, but you may be tipping it.

In the end, it becomes a matter of the joy of creating a memorable character and hanging on to what you have left, or maybe just getting another number. Or, as Cyril already knew, he was protected by the terms of his contract that stipulated that if one number was eliminated, it had to be replaced with another. The longevity of his career and power served him well.

Cyril Richard was the dearest of souls. He was tender and patient during the entire rehearsal process. His wife Madge was gravely ill and I believe she died sometime during the run. He totally worshipped her. The Lost Boys particularly adored him. His favorite was David Bean, who played one of the Lost Boys. David's father became Cyril's dresser and Cyril became David's mentor.

One of my favorite things to do was to visit Cyril in his dressing room and drive him mad. "Oh Cyril," I'd say, "can I have your autograph for my grandmother? She would be so honored." He would get all bubbly and florid. "She has loved you so much in the theatre." He would become even more bubbly. "She has loved you since she was just a little girl." Then I would make my getaway. Or I would sit there and ask, "Who is the most talented young person in the theatre today?" No answer from Cyril, just a slight smile. So I would swat something from his dressing table to the floor. "Then who in the show seems to be achieving the heights in the performing arts?" Silence again, but his eyes flashed a sweet avoidance of the question. Bam! Something else would hit the floor. Oh, how I loved to tease him.

Cyril had a memory problem with some of his lines. He would almost get them right which made us laugh even more. We did everything not to break up on stage. He'd say, "Stretch him to the budgets" or "Strap him to the giblets" or "Stock him to the gliddgets." He was a wonderful actor and performer who had directed many operas—his passion. He was truly a man of infinite kindness and patience.

I enjoyed working with many cast members including Joan Tewkesbury, who played the Ostrich (later she would write the famed movie, *Nashville*) and Don Lurio who played the Kangaroo (who became the Jerry Lewis of Italian Television). Don Lurio danced and choreographed and was considered a national treasure by the Italians. I would dance with him again in Paris in Roland Petit's company. Billy Sumner was a favorite of Jerry's and had been in several shows for him. He became a special friend of mine. We played many theatre games together and I always considered him Tiger Lily's right hand. I'd known Billy since *High Button Shoes*. He was a practical thinker and eventually saved his money and bought property on Fire Island and later retired to Key West, Florida.

Recently, I spent time with Bob Willoughby, who has become a world-famous photographer, and his wife Dorothy. They now live in the south of France. We shared photos with one another, past and present. We remembered the pet names for Richard Halliday (Mary Martin's husband) who was 'The Black Pearl' and we called Jerry Robbins 'The Black Crow.' We remembered the magical introduction to Neverland with the dancing trees, the ostrich, the lion, and the kangaroo.

Just before the last preview in New York, Jerry asked David Bean, "Why are you NOT saying all your lines?" He answered, "There have been so many changes, I'm saving them for opening night!"

Even then The Lost Boys began to show a little stubble. Noses and elbows grew overnight. Hair on their legs and chests appeared and before too long their voices would drop octaves.

And our darling Wendy—Kathleen Nolan—grew up and became President of the Screen Actors Guild—a real powerhouse.

My Affair with France
(and My First Affair in Paris)

IN 1958, I SAILED TO FRANCE.

Mirelle's father arrived at Le Havre to meet my ship, the *Ile de France*. He was to welcome me to the Lefebvre household, to Paris, and deliver me to Roland Petit's *Les Ballets de Paris*. Mr. Lefebvre was a jolly, roly-poly man. I was so excited to meet him and hugged and hugged him.

He explained to me that Roland Petit could NOT meet me here at the dock, as the company was still in London. It seems there had been problems between Roland Petit and Buzz Miller, who had had a fit (about what, I'm not sure) but he hit Roland in the head with a chair. ZiZi Jeanmaire, the star of the company, and Roland's wife, had fainted and hit HER head on the rehearsal hall floor. There had been hysteria, drama, hospitals, etc. To add to it all, Buzz was now GONE! So all had to be delayed for a while, including my reservation at the hotel that I was to go to, trunks and all.

Of course I didn't understand his explanation. As it turned out, Mr. Lefebvre did not speak a word of English, and I did not speak a word of French. Mirelle, his daughter, my dear friend and roommate, was back in New

Mirelle, my French roommate in NY, and her father, Mr. Lefebvre, Paris

York in our apartment. She was in a show that was about to go on tour so she couldn't help! We all tried to manage through pantomime. I had Mirelle's bedroom, which was warm and charming. Of course I had confusion about where the toilet was and couldn't ask, so I peed in the bidet, or sink. It seemed to me that there was a separate room for the shower, the bathtub, the toilet, the towels, and the sink.

The family smiled, bowed, and nodded a great deal, exchanging suspicious eye communications about my mysterious comings and goings as I slipped into this room or that one. They couldn't have been more lovely.

One day I was determined to thank them in their own language for all the loving care I was receiving. And let me tell you, I worked hard. I looked up every word in the French dictionary and decided to wait until dinner hour.

As we gathered there at the dining room table—Mirelle's mother, her father, her brother, Bernard, and the maid—I rose, cleared my throat, and began. This just had to be good. "Merci! Attention!" (Smiles all around.) I began.

"*Madame et Monsieur Lefevbre. Je suis trés content! Je suis trés heureux!*" (More smiles and nods.) " I am so content; I am so happy." (So far so good; now tears of gratitude are sliding down my cheeks.) "*Je, Je voudrais baiser tout les deux!*" (Translation: "I would like to fuck both of you!") This story is often told in French, to a stiff mitt. The correct word would have been *embrasser* in order to say what I actually meant—that I wanted to hug them.

I was deeply troubled. I couldn't find Roland or *Les Ballet de Paris*. I didn't know where everyone else had gone. It turns out they were still stuck in England. I had no hotel. I had no instructions and was very grateful for the Lefevbres' hospitality. I had some sort of (you could call it) a nervous collapse. I thought the best thing to do was to head for the Hotel George Cinq, because the people I came over with on the Ile de France were there; all of us had been in first class.

It's a very famous hotel, very posh, on the Right Bank. So I went there and found my way to the bar. I was very nervous. I didn't drink even though on the last night on the boat I might have had a glass of wine or champagne. But I'm not a big drinker, so that was about it.

So I went to this bar thinking I would see some familiar faces. I sat at a table and the waiter said, "Blah, blah blah" in French. I didn't have a clue what he was saying. The woman at the next table said, "I'll have a

Gibson, a dry Gibson." And her friend said, "Oh, why not have an Althea Gibson?" The first lady said, "What's that?" And she retorted, "It's made with a black olive!" They squealed with delight. They were joking about RACE! Today, I would have socked her in the mouth.

But then I didn't understand any of this in English *or* French so I just ordered a Gibson, which looked like a glass of colorless soda water. I drank it quickly because I was nervous. It didn't taste like anything, just a bit medicinal. Shortly after that the waiter said "la,la,la," in French again and I said, "Wee! Whoopee! Wee!"

So *then* he brought me a *second* dry Gibson. By this time I thought one eye was in my ear and the other one was in my mouth. I saw doubles and triples, and everything was prism-like. The whole world was spinning. I became more and more maudlin and more and more *frightened*. I was psychologically ill.

Then I thought I saw a familiar figure in the distance, but it wasn't someone from the boat.

It was Ella Logan, who I knew quite well. With surprising difficulty I got up and earnestly tried to walk a straight line as I knocked over most of the tables in the George Cinq bar trying to get to her. Finally, lurching forward, I grabbed both her shoulders and sagged to my knees, toes pointed inward scuffing the carpet.

"Scuse me,"(kind of liver lipped). "Are you Ella Logan?"

"*Sondra*," she said, "who the hell do you *think* I'd be, Catherine of Russia?"

"Glib, glub, gloob," said I, collapsing into her arms, and then falling at her feet.

Next thing I knew, I was around the corner at the Queen Elizabeth Hotel that Ella was residing in. As I came to, I heard her on the phone with a doctor who was obviously being summoned. I overheard how I was dragged through the lobby of the George Cinq, babbling and wild-eyed, with my bloomers hanging out! (It took me twenty years to walk back into that hotel!)

I must have drifted away again and then come around once more. I heard Ella say to someone on the phone with her 'brogue' (the person turned out to be the jeweler, Norman K. Winston), "the doctor said that's she's so traumatized that we've got to get her the hell out of the country in order for her to come back to rehearse without collapsing and turning to shit!" So this very gracious man who did not know me, but knew and adored Ella (as everyone did who knew her), gave her the money to get me out of France.

Ella took me to Spain to recover for a few days, or more. And that's how I got to Spain. We stayed with Mary Pickford's adopted daughter and her husband. I believe his name was Bud Yorkin or Orkin. Hers was Roxanne. He was the head of some American picture company in Spain. To be perfectly honest, I didn't know *where* I was. I was so turned around it was ridiculous. And anyway, you didn't eat until 10:30 or 11 o'clock at night. We ate vats of garlic soup and I heartily devoured the great food.

In Madrid we went to the Prado. We also went to the bullfights, which wasn't very good for my mental state. One time during a bullfight, there had been a guy who got too over-excited and yelled, "Son of a bitch!" And since that was considered an insult to Mother Spain, the authorities whisked him off to the penitentiary for the rest of his life!

Next was Barcelona. As we were walking down the street in Barcelona one day, Ella suddenly took off. She sprinted as fast as the wind. Bewildered, I ran after her, and finally as we arrived at our hotel she explained what had happened.

"Well, when we stopped for the red light, remember? I had to go the bathroom. I couldn't hold it in *any* longer. And these two *Gendarmes* were behind us, these guys from the army with the big black patent leather hats. I looked down as I peed, I peed on his FOOT!! I peed on his BOOT!! This was after the guy who had yelled, 'Son of a bitch.' And you could go to the penitentiary for that. I realized I had just peed on THE ENTIRE SPANISH ARMY! They could have—and *would* have —put me away! FOREVER! What else could I do?" So Ella had started running as fast as she could!

We saw great Flamenco dancing, and met wonderful Flamenco singers such as Raphael Romero, one of the greats. I was inspired by the music and the dancing. It was truly healing. At that time, Frank Sinatra was there. The first time I saw him, he was sitting on the window, dangerously, on the sill, above the street, legs dangling. He said something snide to Ella from the window. She had recently given a concert with Sachmo in London, which wasn't well received. Ella had opened for the great Louis Armstrong, yet the audience only wanted to hear him. She had a really rough time and had come to Paris to recover from her disappointment. That's where and how I found her.

Sinatra heard Ella was in Spain and invited her to his hotel and she brought me along. Definitely "Old Blue Eyes" *was* blue-eyed. I thought Sinatra was rather smart-alecky. He was unkind to Ella. She had such a mighty singing voice, doing her famed "Finian's Rainbow" on Broadway and everything. And he was such a big star and knew that she was hurting.

I remember that first visit to Spain, not for Sinatra, but for the incredible music, singing, and dancing. We went with the gypsies. Ella, singing Irish and Celtic shanties, which they loved, and me dancing wildly, freely. Just what the doctor ordered. Ella was wonderful to me.

Then I was back to Paris. Although it was only for six months, based on this trip, I became—and still am—a Francophile. I feel like Paris is my second home. I can still wander the streets for hours every day; I feel so connected with this centuries-old city. What is so extraordinary about Paris is the music, the poetry, the literature, the songs, the architecture, the food, and the very sky itself. Although I do not speak the language very well, I feast on the sensual pleasures that echo in my heart. And the friendships I've made there have been lifelong bonds.

It was in Paris that I saw for the first time lovers touch and listen to one another with their eyes. It was in an intimate way I had never seen before or been cognizant of. Men and women sharing a mutual trip to a beauty parlor, just to look good for one another; the enthusiasm of arriving together and leaving together.

The awareness of my own sexuality bloomed in Paris. To go to bed with someone, to make love, was not such an earth-shattering experience and in France it seemed to happen more naturally than in the States. Older women were allowed to be sexy, worldly, emotional—they were allowed to be themselves. So many of the songs sung by Edith Piaf, Charles Aznavour, and Yves Montand were about all aspects of romantic relationships. The attitudes, the concessions, the confessions—the joy and sorrow of living life.

The men in my life were never conquests—neither theirs nor mine—but rather comrades. I am a better comrade, collaborator, and companion than just the 'hot affair' type, though I must admit to a rather large number of comrades, collaborators, and perhaps more than a dash of 'hot' episodes.

Come to think of it—I've slept with a lot of men.

At the same time I joined Roland Petit, I also met Tom Keogh, the American painter and designer. He was tall and slender with the most amazing shock of golden red hair and opaque blue eyes.

Irish? You betcha!

Tom Keogh

An affair?

Yes.

Was I still married? *Uh-huh!*

I was attracted to Tom at once. As I listened to him discuss his ideas for Roland's ballet, *La Fille Aux Yeux Secs* (The Girl With Dry Eyes)—which was being staged for me—I had to scrape my eyes from the floor into his.

Tom had been discovered by Barbara Karinska, the great designer who was one of George Balanchine's costume designers. Tom's success came hard and fast. He was only eighteen years old when he created the costumes Marlene Dietrich wore for *Kismet* (made from hundreds of tiny chains) and went on to create the beautiful ballet costumes in *Daddy Long Legs* and many other films, including *The Pirate*, starring Gene Kelly and Judy Garland. He also had married Theodora Roosevelt, the granddaughter of Theodore Roosevelt, when he was very young. He was revered in the illustration world and designed innovative covers for French *Vogue* and a series of illustrations of Harlem at Easter time that ran in *Esquire*. He and Christian Bérard were the rage. He also designed for stars such as Josephine Baker—sets, costumes, illustrations. He designed for ballet, movies, and opera. This man could do everything! I adored him.

Tom had style, an Irish wit, and possessed real genius. He had a love for alley cat types like me. We had an affair. It was on and off and it lasted for years. However, there was one problem.

He was a bad drinker. He would not violently attack you but he was loaded with surprises when he was drunk. He'd create a scene by hissing insults at you or whoever was in the way. Sometimes he'd remove his clothes and just sit naked at a table in a restaurant—his favorite one or yours. He could be defiant, humorous, and self-destructive.

But when he worked, he was an angel, humming and singing the songs he loved of Germane Montero, Sophie Tucker, Josephine Baker,

Charles Trenet, and Edith Piaf. Once in a while he would do his interpretation of how they currently danced. Or he would surprise you, dressed up in a charming Gulliver-esque costume complete with light velvet britches, a long flowing blouse laced up the front, and shoes with a slight heel and big buckles that he had salvaged from some production.

I'd often find him seated at the drawing board, so unassuming, and paying not the slightest bit of attention to me. He was a real perfectionist—when working on his drawing and designs, he only used the best paper. If he did not like a sketch, he'd destroy it. He liked to give his work away. Tom was generous to a fault. The owners of restaurants were fond of Tom and respectfully hung his paintings.

The costume he designed for me in the ballet reminded me of the clothes I had seen on this extraordinary dancer at Le Bal Nègre, the existentialist dance hall I visited when I first arrived in Paris, just a few days before I met Tom. Le Bal Nègre was said to have been frequented by Jean-Paul Sartre and Simone de Beauvoir during the war. I was listening to a wailing clarinet solo and was told this was "island" music.

The dancer I was watching was more like a creature—her white, white face, black-trimmed eyes resembling a raccoon, and the iris of her eyes so blue—as blue as Tom's. Circling this face was the most beautiful head of flaming red hair like that of an Irish setter. She wore a long loose sweater of faded gray-blue with a darker blue long crepe-like skirt. At her neck was a little fox fur collar and ballet slippers were on her nimble feet. Brigitte Bardot adopted a similar look some time after.

This gorgeous creature out-danced everyone of every color who partnered with her or tried to. In the early 1950's, she was the model for a photography book called *Love on the Left Bank.*

Apparently, when she first came to Paris she was smoking twenty-one pipes a day of opium—a habit she later kicked. But she could drink gin by the glassful.

Her name was La Morte.

During the course of our affair, Tom asked me if I wanted to meet her. He had painted her often since she was one of his favorite subjects. He said that her life story was amazing.

He was right.

It turns out that La Morte's real name was Vali Myers and this famous exotic Parisian character was Australian, not French. When we

La Morte

met, she greeted me with, "Hi Luv. Have a Ga-dey?" We were having dinner at Tom's. I watched her eat her salad with her fingers but "La Morte" even *lifted* her food delicately; her fingers were never messy.

We became friends.

Peanuts from New York City and La Morte from Australia.

At some point she went off to deep Africa. She could have out-danced people there, too. When she returned to Paris she had tattooed a delicate mustache on her upper lip and a few tears on her cheeks. And when she smiled, she sported a gold tooth. On anyone else this would have been disturbing, but on Vali it looked a bit exotic, but beautiful.

Later she became a painter. In the 1980's she moved to Positano, a beautiful town on Italy's Amalfi Coast. She lived in a cottage-like cave with a bed seven feet high so animals could roam freely about. She drew her pictures in a cage-like contraption that could be suspended or lowered from a tree by her husband Rudi.

I am not sure where Vali is now.

And what became of Tom?

He settled on the Upper West Side of Manhattan and for years had lived alone. His lady lived directly across from him on the other side of the park. Her name was Phyllis Mason. She came from well-bred lineage—a Harriman by birth. Phyllis was a very good landscape painter who was generous and took care of Tom then and in his later years.

We remained friends. He was always delightful and charming, and always available for lunch or dinner. He was still drawing and painting, but now it was whenever he felt like it. Quite suddenly he announced he was feeling poorly and became very ill. He tried going to an herbalist in Chinatown but to no avail.

Finally, we got him into a hospital as his illness became more mysterious and serious. He was deeply humiliated that he had lost his bodily functions and had to wear a kind of diaper wrap. My doctor had arranged to get Tom a room in the hospital suited for a 'gentlemen of accomplishment and of no immediate means.'

The last time I saw him I entered his room at Mt. Sinai. He peered at me inquisitively with his opaque blue eyes and asked, "Sondra, what direction am I in?" I was not sure what he meant by this question so I tried a Buddhist-like response and said, "Well, Tom…your bed faces north so you should rest and sleep well."

His eyes met mine. "Sondra," he squinted, "you really are smarter than that. You are one of the smartest people I know. You know I have no direction."

He died on February 15th, the day after Valentine's Day.

In Paris, at American Express, I was standing behind two women with many packages. They were in the midst of some kind of argument. "Venice? Why should we go to Venice? We were in Venice!" "We were never in Venice!" "Oh, yes we were! That's where we had the omelette!"

* * *

Johnny Pineapple

ACROSS FROM THE BRISTOL HOTEL on Rue du Faubourg Saint-Honoré, there was a Hawaiian dancer who was appearing at the *Lido* by the name of Johnny Pineapple. (It *was* his name, honestly!) I was living in a charming room on the ground floor of a hotel on Rue du Cirque. Adjacent to the hotel was a restaurant that made great *piperade* and *pomme frittes*. In the mail I would receive this stuff to bleach my hair, which I would wash in the bidet.

Once I was ill with a bad flu and a great dollop of depression, although almost *all* illness is attributed by the French to the grippe or else it must be your liver.

But back to the story. Johnny Pineapple was appearing at the Lido. This adorable fellow was a "slap dancer."

What is a slap dancer?

When natives do these dances jumping over swords and sabers, they slap their arms and hands against their naked chests, stomachs, and *anything* else that has exposed skin. They beat all kinds of rhythms as they leap about. It can be very dangerous as it is violent and very fast. Since I was sick in bed, Johnny Pineapple came to visit.

I was delighted as he explained to me what slap dancing was. He also offered to show me how it was done. My response was euphoric. Off came his shirt and trousers. Johnny went into his routine, slapping the shit out of himself when suddenly the door to my room opened, revealing the chambermaid. Her eyes widened like she had seen a gigantic spider, her mouth ajar, and then she bolted for her life. I am sure she thought she came upon some bizarre "mating" dance. The scene was straight out of Georges Feydeau.

Hotel Paradiso

I HAD JUST RETURNED FROM PARIS and the *Ballets de Paris*. I was called to audition for *Hotel Paradiso* by one of my agents, the adorable Harriet Kaplan, whose elongated and slightly separated eyelashes made her resemble Minnie Mouse. Everyone adored Harriet and her partner, Lily Veidt, whose husband was Conrad Veidt, a worthy actor from the movies who played svelte *monocled* German types. Both these women were wonderful agents who came out of the great Robbie Lanz offices. They were so different from one another. Harriet was kind of scruffy-looking with a raspy, unanimated voice and a cigarette stuck to her bottom lip. She was constantly either losing the bobby pins from her hair, dropping her earring, or dropping the phone as she was hard at work making a deal. Lily, on the other hand, was an elegant thoroughbred, with just the slightest German accent.

A miracle happened.

Allyn Ann McLerie was auditioning for the role of Victoire and so was I. Victoire was the saucy maid, the soubrette of all soubrettes in *Hotel Paradiso*. The show had been a huge success in London, starring Sir Alec Guinness (whom I proudly think I resemble). As I sat in one of the dressing rooms glancing at the script, trying to make some choices for the reading, Allyn Ann went out on the stage, quickly returned (this is unheard of!) and announced to all of us that she had marched out on the stage and addressed the director Peter Glenville, and the producers Charles Bowden and Richard Barr.

"There is no sense in my reading the part, as the person who is really perfect for it is in the dressing room, and her name is Sondra Lee!"

That was miracle number one.

Miracle number two is that I got the part!

Hotel Paradiso opened in the spring of 1957 at the Henry Miller Theatre. And *Paradiso* was paradise! We, the members of the cast, would stand in the wings and laugh at one another's performances. And there were wonderful performances. James Coco had a tiny part and he was hilarious. Actually, we all were! Angela Lansbury was one of the stars. She wore a wonderful wig and beautiful costumes. Ever so the gracious lady and equally hilarious, Angela has become a lifelong friend. The great clown Bert Lahr—one of the most beloved comic actors in the worlds of burlesque and theatre—was the "big" star. He was genius funny and also known to be a great hypochondriac. If Bert felt a cold coming on, we *all* had to have shots. We took injections of vitamins, liver supplements, cold medicine—you name it! We took the cure and he didn't!

Angela Lansbury and Bert Lahr

Other members of the cast included Vera Pearce, Dougie Byng, Carleton Carpenter, and John Emery—who could cross his upstage eye, the one the audience could not see, and drove us crazy as we tried not to crack up! John also made lip-smacking erotic noises and he chose to make them right when he was standing behind you. At the time he was married to ex-ballerina Tamara Geva (Balanchine's first wife). When we were previewing the play in Washington, he would call *Mother Russia* each night after the show.

Peter Glenville was the director. He was a gifted man and the tidiest director I'd ever worked with; not a bead of perspiration ever, I swear. Osbert Lancaster designed the costumes and sets. I adored my black curly wig that had a spit curl resting on the forehead. The play was a big hit. It was featured on the cover of *Life* Magazine, and received many awards. This Feydeau farce was the hot ticket!

Even so, Bert was a constant worrier, and quite often he could be found counting customers outside the theatre. "Aah dey *buying?*" he would implore. "Aah dey *buying?*"

One evening he beckoned me conspiratorially into his dressing room. He told me I was a star of some importance and that friends of his had seen me dance in Paris. He then bestowed upon me the honor of an 8 x 10 photo of himself, signed, *"Best Wishes for your success, Bert Lahr."* Believe me, it *was* an honor.

Yes, we all had a wonderful time in *Hotel Paradiso*. On most weekends, I would drive up to Connecticut with Angie and her children, Anthony and Dee Dee, who were little kids then, and her son David, who was a little older than the other kids. I believe he was her stepson from her husband Peter's first marriage.

Whenever I'm in L.A., I call Angie and she still makes me feel welcome. Last time I was there, Angie took me to the latest "in" place for lunch. Heads bobbed and mouths whispered, "Who the hell is Angela with?" We shared a mixed green salad, a bowl of soup, and told the best roaringly funny bawdy jokes of the moment. Angela holds her family really close and is united regularly with her brother, Edgar, who is a producer. She loves her gardening, especially orchids. She is a classy, beau-

Angie at her house in Ireland

tiful lady—a consummate compelling professional artist who is unspoiled—an antidote for one hundred divas.

Angie is quite tall, and has a way of looking above your head without eye-to-eye contact. Sometimes people are leery of this but I think it comes from being tall and feeling awkward about her height. Perhaps this is a carryover from her youth. Her husband, Peter Shaw, was a handsome, loving, and elegant man. Gone, now gone.

When you call a star like Angie and leave a message, she calls you right back and it's always Angie on the line. She is physically as stately as Stella Adler, but not the same kind of "razzle dazzle!"

However, I must say that my experience in *Hotel Paradiso* confirmed how I felt about stars. I don't feel you must pledge allegiance to the star by stepping aside or doing *less*. One day, Peter Glenville came back and told me he thought I was working very well in *Hotel Paradiso,* but he also strongly said, "*Unfortunately*, the show was *not* about a young maid whose name is Victoire!" So I learned that an actor must *think* about the character they are playing and not take it further than it's meant to go. Peter was right.

A Guest of the Baron Philippe de Rothschild

PHILIPPE DE ROTHSCHILD WAS A MEMBER of one of the world's most incredible families—the legendary Rothschilds. When I knew him he was a poet, a grandfather, and one of the most successful vintners of the 20th century. He was only twenty years old when he took over the operations of the Chateau Mouton Rothschild vineyards in France. In the 1960's, he created the Museum of Wine in Art on the premises of the estate that houses a priceless collection of art, including the individual wine labels, which were created by famous artists such as Henry Moore, Salvador Dali, Marc Chagall, and Pablo Picasso.

Diana Vreeland, the longtime editor of *Vogue,* once said that her favorite place to go was to be invited to the estate of the Baron de Rothschild in Mouton because of its inherent beauty and the comfort you received as a guest during your visit. I didn't know when I read her article that one day I would be on my way to this fabled place.

I knew that Philippe had raced cars in his younger days

Philippe, before we met

(using an alias name!) at the Grand Prix in Le Mans. I knew he was educated at Eaton or Oxford and was fluent in three languages. I knew that his first wife died tragically in a concentration camp during World War II.

Philippe had been a great ladies man in his younger days. The Baron was a man who never slept much. An injury to his inner ear left him with a constant buzzing sound.

Why am I telling you this?

Because the Baron had been my lover.

How it started, I will tell you later.

Jean-Claude Vignes

FOR AT LEAST THIRTY YEARS OR MORE, I was part of a group that converged at the home of our dear friend, Jean-Claude Vignes. His family had a large, rambling apartment in Paris on Rue Quentin Bauchart. It had been his grandmother's and all the children and their children used it from time to time. We would take turns living there, eating there, or just plain sneaking into it. God, the networking Jean-Claude did for us! You had no idea who would turn up there—Thomas Schippers, Anthony Perkins, all sorts of luminaries.

Everyone adored Jean-Claude. He was connected to everyone and all of us loved him or were *in love* with him. This was the apartment of the squeaky cheese. It was the running joke for newcomers at lunch. When the cheese tray was presented, we told the newcomer discreetly to select a 'certain' cheese (as it was rare and delicious) and when it 'squeaked,' we roared and fell about.

And it was in this apartment where our brains were fed. The tender scenes of trying to understand one another—what we did and wanted to do, could do, tried to do, and simply could not do.

Jean-Claude Vignes, painter

Me at Jean-Claude's, Cannes

Eventually Jean-Claude moved to his grandmother's winter apartment in Cannes in the south of France. Here again we would gather in this haven like a group of children on a sleepover. The first one to rise would start the kettle. We slept wherever we found a bed. We gathered at breakfast around this old wooden table in the dining room, which also contained a small bed and was my favorite place to sleep. Several different languages were spoken although most was in English for my sake!

I can still see the small pitcher of milk, the toast, the China tea, the fresh, pale yellow butter, and the honey from the Alps. I can hear the clinking of china in my ear as the cups and plates were being placed at that table. I can see the open shutters facing the sea, the palm trees in front of the house growing larger each year, and the Wandering Jew plant, ever pruned as I see it climbing up the right side of the shutter so you can't close it. I hear the echoes of people going early to the beach down below.

I asked Madeleine, "Why is the bread so good in France? "

She replied, *"Because there's just a little dirt in it!"*

This was a time of high energy and calmed nerves.

We wandered, painted, wrote, swam, thought, shopped. But at the same time, we still remained on our own, since each of us had our chosen rituals and routines. Part of the morning was spent going to the market on Rue St. Antoine, which was alive with vendors, vegetables, flowers, fruit, cheese, and oh—the almonds still in their jackets. There were herbs, dried fennel for grilling fish, and little packets of herbs to add to couscous. I can still smell the melon from Cavillion. At one o'clock each afternoon the whole area became a parking lot!! I still see all of us walking to our favorite bakery on the Rue George Clemenceau to get croissants and brioche.

It is France where incredible dishes are still made on little stoves and in tiny ovens. It's in the wrist!! Soufflés, tarte tintin, gigot, oh yes! It is the French who can take an instant potato mix, add an egg yolk and spices, and the dish is better than what angels could cook!

Oh! The riot of color and activity. When I 'see' these things and 'hear' these sounds, I think of Jean-Claude often. He was a great painter and a wonderful friend. I miss him so terribly. He died of AIDS in 1996.

Ballets USA – *Spoleto*

I was one of seventeen dancers that Jerome Robbins selected to be in Ballets U.S.A., his new dance company that was to appear at Gian Carlo Menotti's Festival of Two Worlds in Spoleto, Italy in the early 1960's. I was honored to join this exciting, experimental group that existed for two seasons. All of us were different sizes, shapes, and colors.

We had the wonderful Robbins, the composers Samuel Barber and Robert Prince, Reuben Taratunian, the brilliant costume designer, and sets by Ben Shahn. Eventually the company was a huge success all over Europe. When we opened we were practically carried through the streets of Spoleto by people who glorified us and kissed our hands. We were quite the *brouhaha*.

Although we rehearsed a little in New York, we were essentially going to Spoleto to do most of our rehearsing there. Our opening was in June. It was now early April and I was about to board Alitalia Airlines with the others, including Barber and Taratunian. We were all headed on this adventure.

Chandler Coles, who was on the administrative staff of the Festival, escorted our company. We all thought there would be a big party on the plane because of a big bag of stuff that he brought, consisting of cans of rattlesnake meat, a couple of jellybeans, and noisemakers. It was supposed to be festive, funny, and smart.

Shortly after takeoff, the plane developed some kind of trouble and we were forced to land in Philadelphia. Alitalia then gave us little coupons so we could have a free sandwich or a snack. But we turned up our noses. Eventually we all nibbled on a donut and waited three hours in Philly for the plane to be fixed.

When we embarked, it was a new plane and we didn't have the entire plane to ourselves anymore. We just had a rather large section but we still had to share the plane with others. So we got ourselves comfortable in the way that only dancers can. We changed our clothes in the middle aisle because there was nowhere else to change. Of course after all this, we needed to change into our more comfortable clothing such as flannel leg warmers and tights. We were feeling quite cramped so we were trying to do our extensions. We put our feet up on the seats, rubbed one another's feet and backs, all dancer stuff.

We were getting rowdy. We heard the announcement in Italian: "Take your seats. We're about to take off." We returned quickly to our activities of stretching, talking, laughing, and visiting one another. It was a pretty animated time. The stewardesses started shouting in Italian, "Sit down! Sit down!" And then something back in Italian that in English would have meant, "Oh my god, what the fuck do we do with them?"

Ballets USA: Wilma Curley, Patricia Dunn, Sondra Lee, Gwen Lewis, Erin Martin, Barbara Milberg, Beryl Towbin, Joan Van Orden, Tom Abbott, Bob Bakanic, John Jones, John Mandin, James Moore, Jay Norman, James White and Todd Bolender

Blissfully, we didn't understand them. But hours and hours went by and we realized that we had not been served food. It was already six hours into the flight and we were over the ocean without a bite to eat—not one morsel! So we called an Equity meeting and demanded a hot dinner or hot anything no matter what they had to do or where they had to land or else we were going to jump off the plane.

We were a pain in the ass. But hungry dancers are dangerous. We figured out that in Philadelphia they forgot to put enough food on the plane for the journey.

Me and Glen Tetley, *Music for a Farce*, Paul Bowles, composer; Tom Keogh, costume and set; John Butler, choreographer

And then…after all of this…we hit a terrible storm.

The plane was rocking and dipping and soaring and snoring and huffing and puffing and pouting and whimpering and the stewardesses once again were screaming, "Sit down. Ah Fohngoo, sit down!" I still have the faint image of Reuben or Sam Barber trying to get their pants down so they could inject a suppository to keep them calm. By that time we couldn't even get into the bathrooms.

We arrived at three o'clock in the morning in Rome to a motley group of press people, shivering in the cold morning air with their television cameras and movie lights. We looked like a bedraggled group of inmates who escaped from a loony bin. Still, we waddled down the gangplank, waved, and were promptly loaded onto ancient buses on our way to a place called Spoleto. It struck me as so 'off the wall' and funny as I looked at our bedraggled group that I started to whistle the tune to *The Bridge Over The River Kwai*. Everyone whistled and laughed…and laughed…and laughed.

Spoleto is about an hour and ten minutes from Rome. When we arrived, none of us were whistling. We had no idea where we were and we had to start rehearsals. What an introduction!

Yet, Spoleto turned out to be an enchanted place. A great, old town with buildings mostly made out of stone and great sites such as Lucrezia Borgia's castle, the Aquaduct, and Hannibal's Arch. The plan was that each year great artists would arrive to 'do their own thing' in this wonderful, magical place. Luchino Visconti came and directed *La Traviata*, accompanied by busloads of pretty boys. *Night of the Iguana*, by Tennessee Williams, was presented at Spoleto for the first time as a one-act. I called Charles Bowden, one of the producers of *Paradiso*, to get the rights and make it a full-length play. He bought the rights and there it was—Patrick O'Neal, Bette Davis, Margaret Leighton, and Alan Webb. Composing, conducting, writing, painting, choreography—everyone wanted to be part of Spoleto. It was an incredible meeting place of different languages, different styles. At one point, everyone who was truly an artist came there or wanted to.

It was Gian Carlo Menotti's dream come true to present The Meeting of the Two Worlds—Festival dei Due Mondi—to the world itself. And we were all a great success.

Scott Douglas, me, Carmen de Lavallade, Glen Tetley;
second row: Paul Sylbert, Arthur Storch, Bambi Linn

Gloria Swanson

WHEN I WAS WITH JOHN BUTLER'S COMPANY for the second season on our way to Spoleto, the *grande dame* of the silent movies (and later *Sunset Blvd.*) —the great Gloria Swanson—was in first class. Carmen de Lavallade and I would wander in and take a peek. Much to our surprise, she showed up in Spoleto and disappeared. Later, Michael Cacoyannis—the Greek filmmaker best known for his film, *Zorba the Greek*—told me the story. He had approached Gloria Swanson to play a part in this movie he planned on doing. After the initial meeting in Spoleto, they were to meet again in Rome shortly after the opening of *The Trojan Women*.

When he arrived at her apartment or suite, she received him covered in gold lamé, looking glamorous as hell. As Michael began to describe the character to Gloria, she realized she was wearing the *wrong* costume. Cleverly, she began to unwrap herself. Michael was fascinated watching the process. He said by the time he left her she was scrubbing the floor. The role he had considered Gloria Swanson for was won by the wonderful Lila Kedrova in *Zorba* with Alan Bates and Anthony Quinn.

Don't you just love show business?

Claire Bloom

HOWARD AUSTIN AND GORE VIDAL had an apartment in Rome on the Via Giulia. Howard was a great cook and wrote T*he Myra Breckenridge Cookbook*. Claire Bloom and I were visiting for lunch. We had come from Spoleto, where we had been appearing in the *The Trojan Women*. After we left Gore and Howard's, we developed an intense case of the itches, really bad. Unfortunately, all four of us had caught fleas and we had to be fumigated. The apartment on Via Giulia also had to be fumigated. Sometimes fleas take over the city of Rome big time.

Claire was married to Rod Steiger back then, and they had taken a house in Auriella. Claire's mother was staying with them, as was their daughter, Anna (now an opera singer), who was then a baby. I believe they met while appearing in *Rashomon*. At the time, Rod was married to a lovely red-headed actress, but the marriage fell apart when he met Claire.

Billie Allen, a wonderful dancer/actress/director, later married the composer Luther Henderson. Billie and I had been in Marc Blitzstein's Reuben, Reuben *together. The phone rang.*

It was Billie. "Sondra, how would your mink stole like to go to Berlin?" Who could say no?

* * *

Mouloudji, Mouloudji

IN NEW YORK IN THE 1950'S, foreign films were the rage. It's hard to believe that many of them were shown on 42nd Street (before it was reborn) but I, for one, was glad that they were. The Apollo Theatre was a great place to watch a foreign film. Right around the corner on 8th Avenue was the Stanley, a small theatre with a beautiful baroque façade that is now a strip show place. The Stanley presented primarily Russian films such as *The Stoneflower* and the classic *Ivan The Terrible*. The French and Italian films were housed at the Apollo and often at the Thalia, which was uptown on 95th Street. The theatres weren't as rowdy as they are today. I would go with my egg salad sandwich from Horn and Hardart's and gobble up food while watching these incredible films.

I knew I had to watch these films. Only in New York could you find out what it was you needed and then know where to go to get it, like the Film Forum with people like Bruce Goldstein and Karen Cooper or Dan Talbot at Lincoln Plaza Cinemas. I hadn't studied languages, but I was curious and driven to watch these stories and to watch the actors and how they worked. I remember two films specifically: *La Boheme* and *Nous Sommes Tous Des Assassins* (We Are All Murderers), a classic French film about capital punishment. It's about a solider named René who had become so used to killing during the war that even when it was over, he couldn't stop and was ultimately tried for murder.

This actor/singer/writer/painter who played René had been discovered by Jean Cocteau as a young pied-noir (Algerian). He had just one name he used—Mouloudji.

Although I had experienced at a tender age some of the heavy-duty types in New York who were sophisticated, wise, and successful, at this time I still had not had the opportunity to meet some of the European men I would eventually go bananas for.

So let me cut to the chase.

Time passed. I was in Rome. I had already traveled a great deal. I was dining at a famous restaurant—Otello's on Via Condotti—known for its cannoli. Otello's has a beautiful outdoor dining area in the rear and I found myself sitting next to this man, but I could only see his back.

Could it be? I questioned myself. He was wearing his traditional uniform; a black v-neck sweater, a white shirt with an open collar, and black pants. The French seem to have a great penchant for this look and I remembered well the man in this particular uniform. I leaned forward close enough to touch him, but of course I was discreet.

Suddenly I was wordless.

It…was…oh…my…God…argh…ahhhh…goo…goo…ga…! It was MOULOUDJI!!!

I was blushing. My eyes were bulging. I looked like a poisoned dog with desire; a frantic groupie who was drugged by the man and this sensual atmosphere. Here I was in the midst of artichokes, red and yellow peppers, tomatoes, sausages, a cornucopia of salads, pasta, and beautiful wines. And I had temporarily become a Neanderthal.

I had listened to his songs and seen his movies for quite some time and I had collected information about him with reverence. He was an award-winning writer, a respected painter, and of course the adored singer of songs about life and love. The French loved him. I knew so many of his songs well, including *Comme Un Petit Coquelicot* and *The Deserter* (which was written by Boris Vian, a fine playwright and poet who died a few years later at the premiere of his movie, *I Spit On Your Grave*).

A little while later I received a letter from my closest friend at the time, Madeleine Carbonnier. At this time Mad (her nickname) was working for Fontana Records. She said in the letter that she had a friend who was anxious to know someone in New York because 'he didn't know nobody.' Impossible to believe but she was trying to set us up since she knew him well and was tired of hearing about him from me. Yet this meeting never happened; he was supposed to be in the United States for a concert but at the time the contract 'fell in the water' (which meant down the drain).

However, we started to write to one another. By the third letter, he was already calling me 'his darling' and I returned the sentiment. Then we began to exchange photos. He remembered seeing me in the restaurant a few years before that. He thought I had been a bit strange. And of course I remembered seeing him with my entire body and soul and goo-goo eyes. Yet still been too shy to converse.

Mouloudji and me

We finally met. I was appearing in some show in New York. I was too excited to remember which one as the affair began. It was just swell. We were lovers on and off. We corresponded for a long time. And then we lost contact. He had a child; I got married. Yet we always had a special 'ticket' for one another.

He died quietly in Paris at the age of seventy-one in 1994. And to the very end he was still a beloved figure in France. And still writing and painting. Today we don't really have this sort of consummate artist. Tony Bennett might come close, but Mouloudji possessed *poetry*. In his life and in his music, he was simply incredible.

Goodbye, mon amour. Goodbye old friend.

The Beginning of the Baron and Me

I FINALLY MET HIM AGAIN.

I'd been howling about it. Fantasizing for a while. Now that he had become a widower … for four years … now that he was coming to the States—I was beside myself.

He had plans to go to the theatre with my darling friend, John Butler, the choreographer, and his friend Mel and asked if I was free to join them for dinner.

Yes—me, John, Mel, and THE BARON.

I was beside myself. They suggested Barbetta's on Theatre Row since Philippe wanted to be close to the theatre. It was raining so I assumed it was also cold.

Wrong. I wore a three piece wool chalet outfit plus a shoulder bag and an umbrella. Although I was pleased with my appearance, I was hot and late.

When I entered Barbetta's, I asked for Mr. Dwork's table.

Blank stares.

Until I said, "Oh, Philippe…The Baron's table."

Then the bowing began. I was practically carried to the table. It was off in a corner but a focal point of the room. I begged their pardon for being so late. And they were not amused. Promptness was meaningful to the Baron.

His hands were a golden tan. The shape of his fingers was beautiful and his hands were so expressive. The color and texture of his skin was smooth and creamy. His grey-blue eyes flashed with wit and intelligence. Out of a bit of self-consciousness I said, "Do you know I am your new life's companion?"

We all laughed. I wasn't tense anymore. The waiter asked something in French or Italian and I answered in French.

"Oh," he said. "You speak French? "

"Not as well as I suspect you speak English," I answered.

The food arrived. It was overcooked and ghastly. We all ate only three bites of our first course. The wine was also ghastly. The Baron chided them for not having Mouton Cadet. They only had his most expensive wines, and so he ordered a German one.

We left in a raging rain yet luckily found a taxi and drove two blocks to the theatre. The play we were seeing was *Strider*. Afterwards, we joined some other people at Rumplemeyer's on 59th Street, which was known for their desserts. It was particularly famous for their ice-cream. During the next half hour I heard one person after another ask the Baron for one *small* favor after another. I listened and remained silent.

At one point the Baron turned to me and said, "And what can I do for you?"

I said, "You're a poet, are you not? Then write me a haiku."

He was amused and immediately embarked on the assignment.

> A shade on her lips
> When?
> Please
> Don't sneeze.

He gave it to me.

"Now what can I do for you?" he asked again.

"Write me another haiku," I said.

And again, he did.

> Mousie, mousie
> Tiptoe tickle
> Tiptoe tickle
> Ear to nose
> On my pillow.

As I arrived home the phone was ringing; it was he.

"Are you engaged Saturday?" he asked.

"Yes," I said.

"Break it," he said.

"No, Philippe, you do it."

And he did.

Then he proceeded to tell me in a most excited voice how pleased he was with his latest invention. He took an ordinary clothesline and put it around the neck of his dog, Rajah, to take him for a walk. He used it as a leash and this thrilled him!

Thus began an affair—uh huh!

In Cannes, after rummaging through the shoe section in one of the chic stores on Rue D'Antibes, I found a great bargain—a black, shiny pair of Yves St. Laurent shoes. I rushed to show them to Asma, our "fashion maven." Her comment? "Darling, these shoes are so OUT, they're IN!"

* * *

Back to the Baron

THE BARON PHILIPPE HAD EXTENDED an invitation to me to visit him and I had his phone number in Mouton so that all the arrangements could be made.

Jean-Claude phoned for me from his tiny apartment on Rue du Dragon in Paris and asked to speak to the Baron personally. He almost giggled gleefully but before he had a chance the Baron was on the wire. Traditionally, if you were given the number it is because he would love to speak to you. But when you receive an invitation, the dates must be kept. There are no second chances.

"Wednesday, 10:00 a.m., she will be fetched at the airport," he said to Jean-Claude. "Okay? Okay?"—his favorite expression.

I thought to myself, what kind of present do you bring this man? Wine? Cheese? A little Danish? A knick-knack from the Ming Dynasty? What? *You had to be kidding to think he needed anything!* In my luggage I had a sponge in the shape of an American ham sandwich: it was a smash at Jean-Claude's!! Why not? And off we went—Jean-Claude and I—to the south to Cannes.

Asma's car looked like an old gypsy wagon as she and Jean-Claude drove me to the airport in Nice. Jean-Claude was dressed in casual jeans and Asma was dressed in her usual wonderful gypsy concoction. As for me, I chose to wear a gray cotton pants suit—not wanting to look too dressed up but certainly not wanting to appear in shambles. However, I was carrying a huge canvas army duffel bag. Yes, that's how I travel.

Suddenly I'm scared.

I board the plane for Bordeaux, an uneventful trip.

The chauffeur is at the terminal, holding a white cardboard sign. And what does it say? MOUTON. I felt like I was going to Grossinger's in the Catskills but not as a dancer, as a dutchess!

We grapple over the luggage. He wins…graciously. I jump into the front of the car with him and he is amused. The conversation consists of bad French from me and worse English from the chauffeur.

Me: Combien the kilometers a le Maison de Baron?
Him: Pardon?
Me: Le Baron il est la?
Him: Il est la.
Me: A long trip? A Mouton?
Him: Bon.

We pass through several villages. We arrive in the village of Pauliac. We enter a long road and as far as the eye can see there are rows and rows of vines, overwhelming in their orderliness. In the distance I can see that at the end of the road, there's a black wrought iron gate. To the right of the entrance is a beautiful Brancusi sculpture.

This is certainly Tara. A French *Gone With the Wind*. I am wide-eyed. What do I say? "Wow."

With lightning speed, we're out of the car and I start running after a young man wearing black pants, a white shirt, and a gray-and-black striped apron. I have now been whisked to the second floor of the estate and the young man has been replaced by two maids in white uniforms. (At this speed, it feels like I've been rushed to an emergency room!)

My clothes have been instantly put into drawers and a closet. I think, "Thank goodness my underwear is clean."

The doors close. I am now alone, amused and shaken at the same time.

I eye the room. It's covered in a beautiful cloth of birds and flowers. It's everywhere. On the doors, shades on the windows, and the walls. There is one single bed with linen sheets to the floor. The pillows are both large and small. The room holds a combination of two orchid plants, one azalea, and two exotic, lush, large green plants. There's a fireplace and a little table with a record player and records—Mozart, Louis Armstrong—a very eclectic collection.

The bathroom is white, clean, and simple with good, deep towels, a robe, new soap (Roger & Gallet), and above the tub is a small lamp on

the wall covered with a shade with the same fabric from the bedroom.
 This place is magnificent.
 The phone rings.
 Nerves again.

The Baron: Is all well? Has everyone taken care of everything? Good. Do as you wish. Tootle around in a car if you want. Everyone here can do as they wish. Lunch is at one thirty. Drinks are in the park across the way. Okay? Okay?
Me: It's all wonderful. Thank you. Thank you. I can't wait to see you. Where are you?
The Baron: I'm working with my architect to make things simple and elegant. No easy task. Bye-bye.

I hang up. I'm feeling the rhythm of Mouton and remembering what the Baron told me when we met in New York. I say it out loud to myself. "You don't know me until you see me at Mouton. It is my real home. It is me."

My eye catches something to the right of the phone. It's a card with the names and numbers of the rooms. Ten rooms, nine bedrooms in Grand Mouton; seven bedrooms in the Petit Mouton, which is a bit smaller and is the original house just across the way. I look out the window and see a man with a wooden rake making a fresh design on the gravel road. A white pigeon flies by and the sky is simply beautiful. There are vines of grapes for miles and miles.

I remember writing these words while I was still there.

> The cuffs of his shirts
> the tone of his skin
> the hair and mutton chops
> the shape of his fingers
> silk-silk-pink shorts
> heating pad
> the lavender lilies
> great rushes of words
> elegance
> standing in the corner
> Perrier

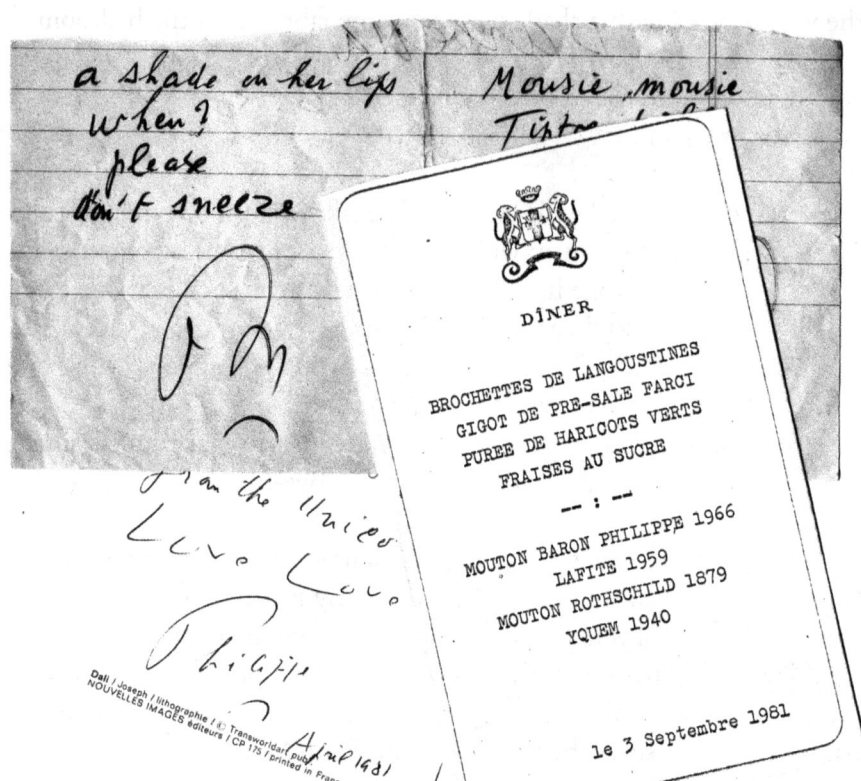

Dinner and haiku (I stole the menu)

When I returned to Nice after this incredible trip, my buddies met me at the airport with a big sign in large letters that said ROTHSCHILD and on the ground was a path of yellow rose petals strewn about. I laughed, I cried; I wet my pants.

One Night in the Sixites

I PHONED MY FRIEND PATSY BRODERICK (the mother of the future Matthew Broderick) to ask her if she wanted to visit "the Beatniks." Jack Kerouac was intrigued with me. We had been introduced at Gian Carlo Menotti's, a composer best known then for his opera, *Amahl and the Night Visitors*. Kerouac was thinking about writing a play for me to do at Menotti's Festival of Two Worlds. At the time, I was rehearsing at the "Old Met" which was on 41st Street. This was my first venture after tearing my Achilles tendon while in *Ballets U.S.A*. My re-entry into dance was performing in John Butler's *In the Beginning*, which was about Adam and Eve. I played the Serpent; the Met Corps de Ballet was my tail.

Now that's another story.

So back to Jack Kerouac. I phoned Patsy Broderick and asked her if she wanted to join me for an evening with the 'notorious' Beatniks, as I had just been invited to "their place." We were hysterical about what we should wear. Colored tights were the newest hip thing in fashion even though dancers wore them for classes every day of their lives. Dancers were responsible for new fashions—they usually are. Go figure! Tights, leg-warmers, the way they apply their makeup; the list goes on and on.

We went to this address way, way on the east side. Avenue B, Avenue A or Avenue C—something like that. When we arrived, they were sitting in the kitchen, all quite courtly. Jack Kerouac, Peter Orlovsky, Allen Ginsberg and Gregory Corso—who had a "w" problem—a kind of lisp like Barbara Wa Wa. We were thrilled and frightened and expected something to happen but had no idea what it was supposed to be.

There they were.

I remember someone got up and banged his head on the birdcage that was hanging from the ceiling. I remember that the refrigerator door had a cutout of Keats and Shelley pasted on it. Frankly, I was too out of focus to recognize who was Shelley and who was Keats. Later on we all sat down and watched James Mason in *Odd Man Out* on TV and ate cream cheese and raisin bread sandwiches. No heavy duty drugs, rapes, or misconduct of any kind. Just a sweet evening at home: although Gregory Corso *did* leave during the movie for a brief time and re-entered dressed as "Little Lord Fauntleroy" wearing a wig with Dutch Boy bangs, straight on the sides. But nothing seemed out of place. They were "the Beatniks."

The play Jack had written for me was about some girl who goes into a diner on Sixth Avenue and is stuck in her behind with a hypodermic needle. Then there was music and something about fried eggs—we never did it.

At another time Jack was drunk on my sofa. Someone made a remark that he was so boozed that he probably couldn't even think. Kerouac suddenly sat up and said, "Test me!" The guy said with a smirk, "Spell hippopotamus." Jack's eyes were bright and red like a rat's lit out of the dark; he sat straight up and spelled it perfectly—H-I-P-P-O-P-O-T-A-M-U-S— then he fell back in a stupor.

Oh, everything was so exciting.

Oh, everything still is!

The One and Only Billy Rose

I MET BILLY ROSE AT A PARTY in the Chelsea Hotel at the home of the composer Virgil Thompson. The food at Virgil's was always delicious and the place was bursting with musicians, painters, poets, and dancers.

I had just come from a dance class that had run very late. At some point I was introduced to a snappy, older guy. I felt his energy and terrific sense of humor. He asked, "Where are all of these guests from?"

I said, "Paris, Spain, Texas, and Los Angeles—everywhere." When he asked me where I was from, I said, "I just came from unemployment." Well, he was mine.

"Just call me Billy," he said. "Where would you like to go at this late hour?"

Without hesitation, I blurted, "The roof of the Ziegfeld Theatre!" So off we went to 54th Street and Sixth Avenue. It had a series of small rooms that might have once been offices. The walls were camel-colored and all that remained were borders left from the paintings and photographs that had once been there. Billy pulled back a curtain and there it was—a view of the entire Ziegfeld stage below.

Billy was cunning. He thought he could buy anything or anyone he wanted. One evening, he picked me up at my apartment on West 34th Street and met my little Yorkie, Maude. He wanted to buy her. "Are you kidding?" I said indignantly. "Absolutely not! She's mine! But I know Swen Swenson, and he raises Yorkies." Off we went to Swen's.

Billy bought a Yorkie, already grown and trained, as he wanted no part of that preliminary stuff. Her name was Zenobie but Billy changed it. When he called her by her new name she was bewildered and confused. A few weeks later I asked about the little dog. I was told the kitchen door was a swinging one and that 'what's her name' didn't clear it fast enough and she died.

What else can I say about Billy and his sense of entitlement?

If he wasn't able to buy a must-have painting by one of the old masters, he'd buy a copy. Half the books on his shelves were fakes: they were painted to resemble rare collections of books. However, he was a good sport and had a great sense of humor. He could also be very generous (this is what he told me!). Often when he wanted to get into that big limo of his with his chauffeur, I would insist that we walk. And sometimes he would, grudgingly.

Today his house is now the property of R. Brinkley Smithers, a recovery house for alcoholics. The bathroom was built for Eleanor Holm, the swimmer (who was his wife after Fanny Brice). It still has her figure etched on the glass shower stall.

We only had sex at my apartment, never his. He was not a lover but he could be good in bed. I once asked him, "How much money do you have?"

"Seventeen million," he responded. Then his eyes became beady and suspicious. "On paper, that is." Maybe he thought I had a plan.

After Billy died there were endless arguments within his family about where he should be buried—maybe in a mausoleum. His body was left on ice for a very long time. Yet another Billy Rose production.

In his early days when he was a secretary for the financier Bernard Baruch, he asked Bernard what made a song a hit. Baruch said words that have two of the same letters, as in *"ee"* or *"rr."* So Billy wrote *Barney Google* (with the goo-goo-goo-ga-ly eyes). It became a big hit.

His Billy Rose Theatre came with instructions—you couldn't eat in the theatre. You couldn't move this or touch that—everything was a Billy Rose 'something.' He *was* a Billy Rose production!

Hello, Dolly!—*Previews in Detroit*

Today, November 22, 1963—The President of the United States was assassinated in Dallas, Texas.

I'll never forget it. The news reports announced he was shot in the head. The cast of *Hello, Dolly!* had assembled for rehearsal at the Fisher Theatre in Detroit. Then we received the rumor that we were to be sent home. I overheard Carol Channing *babbling* on the phone about "pressing on." It may have been to the Johnsons, as they were friends of hers. There was Eileen Brennan, with her large pink curlers sticking out all over her head—her eyes rimmed red and cheeks wet with tears.

Charles Nelson Reilly was talking about nothing. Occasionally he'd say something like, "What mother could have a boy like *that*?" (referring to Oswald). Mike Stewart was wide-eyed with disbelief. "What will happen now?" he murmured.

I could not bear to think of the future of the country. The nuclear age—the terrifying atmosphere we lived in. All of this as I watched my little dog Molly innocently playing with her toy.

I called my friend James Baldwin, the writer, on the telephone in New York. I said, "Maybe we won't be dependent on one person. Maybe it will come to be that people like Kennedy will still mean something. They can't be stopped—their force cannot be stopped! Life's *force* cannot be stopped.

Jimmy said, "Sondra, it's a gray day. I hope it rains gently, for him, you, for me. We will grow stronger. His blood—ours now."

My heart slumped. There I was in Detroit, a racist town. Our friends were away, not here in Detroit, but—home! All of us were saddened and sick. I was feeling alone. I kept stroking my little dog, whose eyes looked upon me with total unconditional love. This calmed me a bit. We stayed huddled around the radio backstage as if it were a pot-bellied stove. I called Jimmy Baldwin again. "Go get some groceries and be gentle with yourself," he said.

Months later, the Kennedy family saw *Hello, Dolly!* in New York. We had already opened and were a smash hit. The secret service came backstage at the theatre. They were recording any sudden sounds or shots. Later the family came backstage and we gathered and bowed like they were royalty, which they are. But I really wanted to hug them and hold them close. They were so brave, and so classy.

A Gift From Gower and Marge

GOWER AND MARGE CHAMPION (his wife and dancing partner since their early teens) gave us opening night presents that made us feel like we were going to be on Broadway for a long time. Tea pots filled with autumn flowers for the dressing room and small personal gifts such as silver combs from Jerry Herman and clocks and cheese from Mike Stewart. One feels the exhilaration and the love, even after all the hysterical scenes and accompanying anguish, the firings and replacements, the dialogue cut from scenes, the songs cut, the dances cut, the solos!

When the first reviews of *Hello, Dolly!* came out during the opening night party, I was so touched to see Marge and Gower hold each other and start the first dance alone on the floor. Both elated and exhausted, their bodies knew one another so well. I can still see Gower with his pencil-thin body, slightly pigeon-toed. He was handsome and had a tap dancer's body, with a tight jaw and great teeth. Gower often had crushes on his leading ladies. Marge *chose* to be blind in one eye, as the saying goes. She had been there before.

They divorced after *Dolly*. After Gower died, Marge and I became close friends.

Hello, Dolly! *and Eileen Brennan*

During *Hello, Dolly!*, Eileen Brennan and I, unbeknownst to each other, had exclusivity of the dressing room in our contracts. We were great buddies at the beginning of the show. The Merrick office assumed it would be perfectly all right if it was a large dressing room that Eileen would have one side and I'd have the other. We never argued about it until one day, after some friction, Eileen said, "I have exclusivity of my dressing room so I'm going to have one."

I retorted, "I also have exclusivity—and so I will have one!"

At that time, the Shubert Theatre did not have enough dressing rooms. The first thing they did is put up a curtain to separate us. We said it wasn't good enough and threatened lawyers and agents. So they had to put in a new wall, which they did; to this very day, I believe the wall still exists. But I think the show *The Producers* finally took it down.

The only thing is, I ended up with the radiator and Eileen ended up with the air conditioner. All winter she was freezing and all summer I was dying from the heat. When I think about this situation, I still laugh. You really don't care too much about those particulars at the beginning of your career, especially in the older theatres, since there's nothing grand about them. Out front they can be beautiful surrounding the proscenium, although the backstage area can be just plain tacky!

A Gift From the Star

WE WERE TO RECEIVE CHRISTMAS GIFTS. Our imaginations took over because we were asked in advance what our initials were, so of course everyone thought *sterling* as in silver. Then we heard not only was it coming from Neiman Marcus but that it was coming from Carol Channing, the star.

The Neiman Marcus boxes began to arrive. They were piled up to the ceiling in dressing rooms. And we thought, "Oh, God, this is great." We tore off the wrappings. I opened mine. It was the largest pair of white bloomers I had ever seen. In the right hand corner were the initials S.L.

Bibi Osterwald's said B.O.!

They were devastatingly large. The men received skinny ties with their initials stamped in white paint.

At first, when everyone found their packages in their dressing rooms you could hear squeals of delight as they tore open their gifts. Then a slight pause and silence. Yes, a resounding silence in the theatre. And then hearty laughter. Everyone thought it was the greatest joke of the season.

This *was* the present—no joke involved.

I marched into Carol Channing's dressing room to show her, and I said, "Carol, I want to keep these forever."

And she replied, "Oh, that's just lovely."

And so I framed them.

Just before a lilting waltz around Dolly Levi, which accelerated into a spinning spirited exit, Chet and I ready in the wings...Suddenly, he yawns. "Sorry, I've been out balling all night!" I sez , "Big deal!" (Music cue starts) "I have a lover and we did it too!" (Entrance music starts, whirl, whirl) (in my ear) "BOWLING! Sondra, I was BOWLING all night!!!"

* * *

Me and Ginger

GINGER ROGERS TOOK OVER THE ROLE of *Dolly* from Carol Channing. One night she confessed to the audience that she had forgotten her line and told them to "just wait a minute." She would leave the stage and return to report to them that she "had it now." I would cringe with humiliation for her, but the audience just loved her for letting them in on it. She did this each time she forgot!

For the public, Ginger dressed in old movie star clothes. She really didn't give a damn how she dressed when she was home alone. But for the public, she went all the way, including full makeup. She had thick arms and a very athletic body with lots of freckles. She loved golf with a passion and played religiously. She was almost a most dedicated Christian Scientist. And she spoke from the side of her mouth, like when she was playing Roxie Hart.

The concept she had of herself was the 1930's view of a goodhearted shop girl who could get tough if she had to. The story (her mother Lela told me) is that when she got married the first time, the grips and carpenters held up their hammers like a military wedding and Ginger marched happily beneath them.

I remember she had a scar across one ear that had been cut by an earring many years ago. I also recall that Gower Champion had cut part of my dance in *Hello, Dolly!*, referred to as the "Avon Comedy Four," and gave it to Ginger. She couldn't really dance anymore and it was difficult for him to choreograph numbers for her. Although this was painful for me, it was easier for him. He also asked me to tour with Ginger for a short time. This time on tour he gave me the section back. The entire cast gathered in the wings the first night I did it again and applauded; Ginger did, too. I had always received spontaneous applause.

On the night we closed in San Francisco, Ginger made a speech about me and informed the audience I was leaving the show. I took a curtain call alone and received a standing ovation. I was overwhelmed with emotion and couldn't stop weeping. She truly was a good egg, and a good sport, as I observed her in her later years. I heard that she was in New York promoting a dress line for JC Penney. I phoned her at the hotel she was staying at and she returned my call.

A good egg, a survivor. Three husbands; marriage was not her thing!

More On Hello, Dolly!
(or The Long Run)

I RUN INTO A FRIEND ON THE STREET.
"Hey Sondra, you look marvelous. How are things?"
"Fine, just fine."
And the friend, "How are you?"
A lot of nodding. A lot of teeth.
"What are you doing now?" asks the friend.
Then it happens. My eyes go darting to the pavement.
"I'm in *Dolly*," my eyes are now concentrating on his toes.
"You mean you're still in *Hello, Dolly!*" exclaims friend standing still as in stilettos.
I stand there mumbling words something like, "(mumble) pardon," "(Mumble) new drapes," "(mumble) Merrick," (mumble) hate it."
But all the time my mind is saying, "Why do I feel so ashamed before a friend? "
"You must be going out of your mind by now," says the friend.
I give a pallid smile in friend's direction and a furtive glance to God. By this time I am barely audible.
"It's hard, very hard." I sigh deeply.
Friend becomes more animated as I see a gleeful glimmer glide into the corner of his eye. He gives me a nudging, knowing wink. "How's Ginger?" Now he's even more intimate.
"She's fine, just fine" (pause) "I'm sorry...I like her very much. She works hard and the audiences love her."
Buses and trucks go through the silence.

I blush and giggle and find myself sincerely telling and promising friend that I will be leaving the show very soon. "Very, very soon."

I'm not exactly sure for what-or-why but I've said the right thing because friend embraces me.

"Good," he says. "I'm glad to hear it. You're too good to be wasted like this."

Friend waves good-bye and I take refuge in an outdoor corner phone booth. I call my buddy Patsy—no answer. I phone my friend Mary—she answers.

"Mary, this is another of my life and deaths." She laughs and then I laugh. "Mary, I'm wilting with shame." I tell her what happened. She says come over for coffee, we'll discuss it, and adds that on the way I should bring her milk.

Almost end of story.

The light changes. I cross the street and head up Central Park West. I stop to buy milk. The clerk asks, "Are you in a show?" I nod yes. "I saw you Thanksgiving; it's a wonderful show." I brighten. "That *Hello, Dolly!* is really great. My wife and I want to see it again. That Ginger Rogers is really something and you're all terrific."

"Thank you, thank you."

End of short story.

Perhaps there is a kind of contempt that some people have who cannot believe you're still in a show that is happily running. When you think of it, no one ever stopped Ethel Merman on the street and asked, "Still in *Gypsy*?" But what exactly does happen to an actor to make him feel this way? There are many reasons.

I was featured in *Hello, Dolly!* on Broadway as Minnie Fay. I was contracted to be in the show for eighteen months. It had already been over a year and I was becoming slightly berserk. No one can do a show for that amount of time without going slightly bananas or you're above the title, like Hugh Jackman in *The Boy From Oz*. Somehow it's different—star power, privilege.

In a long run—it isn't boredom, but exhaustion. I could often be found walking along Eighth Avenue in my costume between the first and second acts and the stage managers would stop me and say, "Where do you think you're going?"

"I'm going home."

And they would say, "Well, please come back and just try to do the second act."

Once again, I was exhausted, a lunatic, and completely out of it. There are certain pitfalls of a long run—the nightmare of losing your concentration or going up on your lines or lyrics, the panic of repetition.

Here's another—seeing an actor *with alarming speed* becoming too *familiar* in his role, especially older performers who become too protective about certain 'old bits' or 'shtick' that they know will work. But in order to keep a role fresh, the actor must always give this up and find new things or you can throw the baby out with the bath water. In the long run, in order to keep it fresh, you must summon your technique. Performing in the theatre demands DISCIPLINE, INTEGRITY, TECHNIQUE, and of course, TALENT.

Anna Sokolow once said to me on the subway, "Hang on…hang on…How many long runs do you have in a lifetime?"

And now I see—if you're lucky, one, or maybe two at most.
Still, it can remain exhausting and the actor must know when enough is enough. Just like a doctor who's been operating all day, the actor must know when to call it quits and move on.

When a show revolves around a star like *Hello, Dolly!* does—and always will—from the start, the actor is in a vulnerable position. For the featured people, the distortions are ego-shattering. For example, there were three Barnaby's before we even opened. What a heartbreak for a young performer! It takes such bravery to leave a show after that kind of disappointment. And also to try again! Jerry Dodge was the first one who opened on Broadway. We were great friends. Tragically, Jerry died long before his time.

However, the casting in the original *Hello, Dolly!* worked brilliantly even though the featured players weren't given enough to do. As a result, every laugh, every moment was of momentous importance. Kind of like…*coitus interruptus*. And yet it worked: we were told by the world, based on the reactions of the audience, that the show worked.

Certainly I couldn't take more than two years of this show; at one time this is what you would sign up for. It's very different today. The producers are lucky if they get a star for three to six months at the most. Negotiations were a joke compared to what goes on today. It was unheard of for a dancer or a performer to be leaving because they were filming a TV pilot. It was a completely different frame of reference, a different set of values. But this was before TV was such a big deal; it was another whole can of beans.

I truly understand that I belong to the active part of the theatre that produced the last of the great legends—Ethel Merman, Gertrude Lawrence, Mary Martin, Yul Brynner—these were great Broadway stars, musical theatre stars. Carol Channing was truly the last of the great Broadway stars; the end of the line. They all went from one show to another and then toured the country in these same shows. They didn't have TV where you're on one night and then by the next morning everyone knows you. They became more than Broadway stars, for audiences all over the United States saw them perform live and loved them.

Yes, it was a very different time. The passion, the determination, the bravery. You rarely see it anymore in the same way. When you saw a person in the chorus, you knew that in a year or two they would get a larger role and then another larger role. They would serve their time; not just walk in off the street. Those were the rarities.

Indeed, a very different time. Checking into the theatre and putting an 'x' next to your name. The atmosphere becomes familial; another life begins—rituals, factions, competitions, sibling rivalry. The bonding together when an understudy goes on for the first time and the cast being so supportive when they *do* get their chance. Cheers all around!

Even the lights were not the same. We had a real followspot. And footlights were *in the foots*! The orchestra was always in the pit. Today, it can be anywhere it wants to be or even run by a computer.

Even the theatre makeup has substantially changed. We would take two red dots of lipstick (especially in ballet) and apply them to the inner corners of our eyes to open and enlarge them. We wore full stage makeup. Today, it's slightly heavier than what you wear on the street.

Does anyone wear grease paint anymore? It came from a tube. You could build your facial structure, change the shape of your cheekbones, the shape of your nose—whatever you liked. Now we have plastic stuff—rubber stuff—we had little of that. And we put it on all ourselves, even the fake noses. I'm speaking as though this is a million years ago but it's not. Yet *High Button Shoes* was over sixty years ago. Over sixty years, and still so alive to me.

Martha Raye: Vietnam

OUR ESCORT, HOPPER. My affair with the pilot, Pierce. Call it creature comfort! The night the company of officers gave a dinner for me was followed by a huge—and I mean *huge*—air raid! So much of that time becomes a blur. I remember it in snatches. My missing bag, which reappeared, after all my papers had been searched. And my travels with "Maggie" Raye in *Hello, Dolly!* She was a real Green Beret, a lieutenant colonel and a fully qualified nurse. She *needed* a war to pull her chaotic self together. It was then that she became a hero—a brave, gentle, *hilarious* hero.

Maggie behaved like a good daughter for whoever was in command. She saluted and "No sweat, sir'd." The guys loved her, and so did the V.C. They would slip in from the perimeter to see her perform. They all knew who she was. When we toured together with the Green Berets—just the two of us—we assisted in operations in remote places. She was a very good nurse. Maggie loved the servicemen, and they in turn, adored

Martha Raye Saved by Helicopter in Raid

SAIGON (UPI)—Comedienne Martha Raye's battlefront choruses of "Hello, Dolly!" were interrupted by a Viet Cong attack and she and two other performers were plucked to safety by helicopter, the Army reported Wednesday.

Miss Raye was returning from entertaining troops further north of the ill-fated mountain outpost Nui Ba Dan.

She decided to surprise visit to American troops on the crest of the mountain which rises above the flat Tay Ninh province mountain, located 55 miles north of Saigon, resembling from the air

Miss Raye and others in her party arrived for a tour on Oct. ... forming forces detachment...

Me, Green Beret, and Maggie, Vietnam

her. She rarely ate solid food. It was difficult for her to chew.

Her teeth looked like *Chiclets* —a dental gift from her early movie days. And she held the studio responsible.

She loved to drink, to be one of the boys. Maggie liked to have sex, and had it *often*. She would have crushes and was easily led on if a chap adored her and wanted her. She also popped "black beauties," which are *strong* uppers.

Maggie spent thousands of her own dollars calling the families of servicemen who asked her to make calls to their families, especially those who were wounded. In moments like these she was so very dependable.

There was something so *childlike* about her. She possessed a vocal instrument that could touch you. And she sang with every ounce of energy and all the voice she had, even more ardent (passionately) it seemed to me—when she sang *If They Would Be G.I.'s*.

Lastly, Martha Raye had great legs and she was very proud of them. It is ironic that when she was so ill before she died, I heard that they had been amputated.

How I Met Fellini

I had been dancing with John Butler's company in Spoleto, Italy, and also appearing as *Cassandra* in Michael Cacoyannis' *The Trojan Women* along with Mildred Dunnock (*Hecuba*), Claire Bloom (*Andromache*), and Arthur Kennedy. Arthur Kennedy was later fired for a drinking problem. Rod Steiger played *Poseidon*.

It was quite a production. There was a man named Guidarino Guidi who came to the shows and saw my performances. He was one of Fellini's close friends and told him about me.

I was asked to come to Rome to meet Federico, as he was doing this movie or was about to. I was thrilled. I found his voice so quiet and gentle when we spoke. He told me I resembled his wife, Giulietta Masina. I asked him what his movie was about. He said he wasn't sure but he thought of it as *a temperature of the times*. He told me that after I had finished my commitment in Spoleto to go off for a rest. Then he would call when he was ready to use me, which he thought would be for the last scene in the movie—a scene with Louise Rainer. So…I went off to Capri.

Stella

CAPRI.

Right before I began filming *La Dolce Vita* in Rome, I met with Stella Adler in Capri; my glorious friend Stella.

We were in the courtyard at the Guissianna Hotel, where we had gathered her friends for a nightcap. Harold Gomberg, the great oboist, and his wife, Margret Brill, a harpist, joined us. We had danced throughout the evening. I remember Stella danced alone. I believe people were too shy to ask her to dance, so she partnered herself.

Stella was beautiful, alluring, and statuesque. On this night she wore a black pant suit, a white shirt with flowing sleeves, and a bolero. Her pale blond hair surrounded her head like a halo. She often wore fake diamonds and jewels from the Monoprix. They always looked good—perhaps not *real*, but highly theatrical.

We sat at small tables amid the soft night air. When it was time to say goodnight, Stella rose like a hostess at her own party and addressed each of us personally. Included was 'the European kiss' on both cheeks. "Good night, Harold *darling,*" (kiss,

photo credit: Elliot Erwitt

kiss) "this is for you." "Good night," (to the harpist) (kiss, kiss) "this is for you." "Sondra, my darling," (kiss, kiss) "this is for you." And so on and so on. Seated along with us was a very young, quiet, and good-looking man in his early twenties. Stella, her wonderful mouth curled like a naughty cupid (with the very corners resembling the curlicues at the end of a moustache) extended her arm. Enclosed in her hand was her room key. She eased it towards him. Then she stood tall and magnetic—eyes *into* eyes.

"And *this* darling, is for you!"

The next day I saw him and I swear he was transformed into a secure, mature, and even more handsome man!

Stella was truly a great seductress. One afternoon I saw her walking her two shih tzu dogs, Princapie and Mookie, in the center of town. There she was in her big picture hat, licking a mozzarella cheese like an ice cream cone. Stella was someone with a panache that could be spellbinding. Colette would have loved her intellect, wit, voluptuousness, flamboyance, talent, and innate ability to nail phony acting and social behavior, including her own.

Once someone asked, "Are you English?"

Stella puckered her lips. "No, *darling*, just affected!"

That's my Stella.

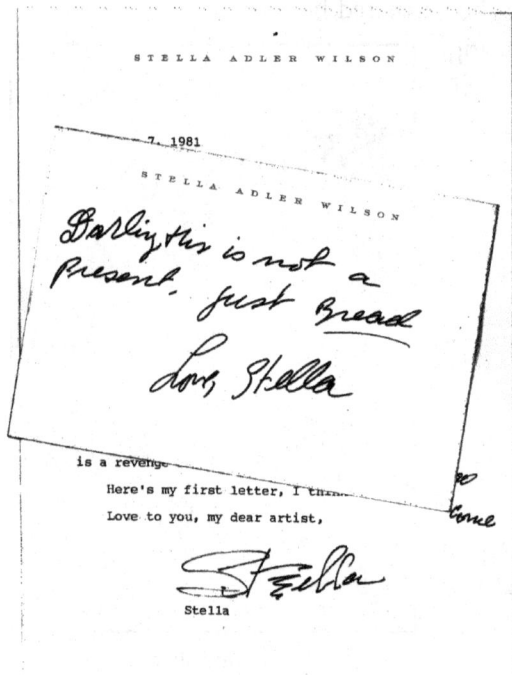

I never felt she liked her hands, her fingers, or her nails. They were rather short and often rimmed with dirt. She wore white gloves almost all the time, preferably long ones. And her hair was always variations of blonde. As the years advanced, her appearance remained theatrical, dramatic, and sexy. Her laugh remained hearty, and was heard often; she enjoyed a good joke and could tell amusing stories. When I married that 'guy' from the Long Wharf (my second husband), as the rabbi was going on during the ceremony, Stella was overheard saying to her husband, "Mitchell, you should have a jacket like the groom's jacket, one with a Nehru collar!"

I will never forget how Stella came to my aid. Up to that point, our relationship had been quite different; she had been my mentor. But in Capri, everything changed. I had been involved in an abusive relationship with a designer during our season in Spoleto, Italy. I found myself pregnant and about to be abandoned by this louse. And I had just committed to taking a role in Fellini's new film, *La Dolce Vita*.

This is a dilemma you would not wish on a helpless puppy.

So I went to Capri on a wild trip in denial. I must admit that for a great deal of the time I sighed heavily, forced weak smiles, and stared into the sea while ordering velveteen two-piece slack outfits that were all the rage. Aside from visiting a glittering grotto and a few social events, my anxiety began to grip me and I got the shakes. So I summoned Stella, who appeared out of the blue like a gift from 'himself' up there. I was foaming and frothing, a spastic frightened figure. I poured out everything to her.

Two beats went by and then: "Darling, you MUST work with Fellini!!!" she said. "I'll see you in Rome next week—everything will be arranged. There is no question you must work with Fellini!" How Stella arranged an abortion in the most Catholic of countries in so short a span of time is something of a hazy and almost erased miracle. I was grateful. The abortion was never brought up again by either of us.

When our friend Larry Blyden's body was shipped back to the states from Morocco, we had to make arrangements for his funeral and inform people about his tragic and fatal car crash. The first person to arrive ready to help was Stella.

After Capri, La Dolce Vita

I was called to go back to Rome to start filming *La Dolce Vita.* I had assumed that I was going to be doing a scene with Louise Rainer. But when I returned she was gone. I asked Fellini why. "Federico, why is Louise Rainer gone?"

"She asked too many questions," he replied.

"Then why did you hire her?" I asked.

"Because she looked like Saint Francis of Assisi!!!"

Each day a car picked me up to go to Fregene—a beach on the outskirts of Rome—or Cinecitta Studios where we shot scenes on the sound stage. Hank Kaufman, an American theatrical agent who lived in Rome, arranged my salary each day.

I ended up in the orgy scene. A real shock to me. Fellini shot the entrance to the scene a few different ways. In one, a car comes to a screeching halt and the actors crept up silently with our faces pushed to the window. The main part of the orgy scene didn't change. As thrilled as I was to work with Fellini, days and days went by without knowing what the hell I was to say, or do, or act. As an actor I needed text!!!!

Fellini adored gay guys and he got two of them out of jail just so they could take part in this scene. He liked oddballs and enjoyed listening to their escapades. On breaks from shooting, he would sit there quietly watching our behavior (some in the cast were inclined to be exhibitionists). And then once back on the set he'd tell 'those' actors to do things without them knowing why.

"Just jump in the pool."

And they would do it!! Whatever he asked. Yet his voice was always gentle and respectful with me.

I was known as 'Sondra, the ballerina from Spoleto.' One day on the set he said to me, "Sondra, after the boys shoot the birds in the cage, maybe they take you upstairs and rape you!"

That was it! I decided this was my last scene in *La Dolce Vita*! As God is my witness, I wrote Fellini a letter—mostly in Chinese figures and just a few words in English—like…"I am, so sorry, exhausted…love you…leaving." Just like that. And the 'ballerina from Spoleto' went back to New York.

La Dolce Vita is a great film. And it was an honor to be there as part of it. What a great director of film Fellini was—one of the best.

When Fellini died I viewed the picture they showed in *The New York Times*. This was the Federico Fellini I remembered. A big man whose hands seemed to dance. His wrists and ankles were small and delicate like in a Botero painting. And there he was—his head thrown back, his expressive hands, fingers apart, and his mouth saying something vital like, "Seize it."

On the Set of Copkiller *and other 80s/90s Films*

I WORKED ON THE MOVIE, *THE ENEMY,* which was later renamed *Copkiller.* Bonnie Timmerman was the one who got me involved in this. The director was Italian and more of a political content filmmaker, not necessarily a director that works with actors. Also, he had a problem with *English.* Nicole Garcia, a prominent French actress, was to co-star with Harvey Keitel. They were all adorable, hard-working actors. Harvey was a detective and Nicole was the caring girlfriend or something like that.

Harvey is an actor who researches his roles thoroughly. He hung out with this detective all day and packed his gat in his sock.

One day we had to shoot for hours in the city morgue right here in New York City. Let me tell you, this was quite an experience. An ambulance arrives almost every three minutes with another body bag. It might as well be a delivery of sacks of coal or clothes, not at all the reality of what you are really seeing. The chill, the smell of formaldehyde, permeates just about everything. It's similar to when you stop smoking and you smell cigarettes on your clothes, hair, and skin. It stays layered in your nostrils!

There were long waits between takes or setting up shots with no place to wander off to. We were in the basement of the morgue. There were rooms with steel refrigerated filing cabinet-looking containers. Just to watch the carriers arrive with the dark plastic bags! After a while, one becomes detached. You kind of *forget* just where you are.

One lasting image I have is regarding the entrance booth. This is where the vehicles arrive. There sat this chubby attendant in his official uniform similar to a policeman's uniform. Rock music blaring from his radio, an open container of Chinese food being scooped up with a pair of chopsticks, and then the food being scarfed down, all as bags revealing some toes with tags already attached to them zoomed by.

We were depressed for the next few days—all of us, including the crew.

Not all locations are in some glorious mystical place with great catering for lunch or dinner, although I do think a clever producer is one who realizes how important instant gratification is on the set. And with a good caterer and goodies on the set during all those grueling hours—especially the night shoots—how grateful you are for chili con carne or hot soup or pizza at four or five in the morning.

Did you know that when your call is for the day—even if it's late in the afternoon—movie people say, "Good morning," so they don't get confused since you all start at the same time? Usually on a night shoot 'Good morning' is when the catering begins—usually around five in the afternoon. Often, it starts with great juicy hamburgers or steak or barbequed chicken. This can be especially hard if you're shooting regular hours the day before. Your entire system gets out of whack. It's so much better if you can have a few days or a week of night shoots consecutively. It not, it can wreck havoc with one's system.

Through the 80s and 90s, I worked on several movies as a consultant to directors, some personal favorites of mine, not all actors.

These are some of the films that I adored working on with some of the directors, cinematographers, editors:

- *Copkiller*, 1983 (Roberto Faenza, director)
- *Places in the Heart*, 1984 (Robert Benton, director; Néstor Almendros, cinematographer; Carol Littleton, editor)
- *Violets are Blue*, 1986 (Jack Fisk, director)
- *Nadine*, 1987 (Robert Benton, director; Néstor Almendros, cinematographer; Sam O'Steen, editor)
- *Light of Day*, 1987 (Paul Schrader, director; John Bailey, cinematographer)
- *Vibes*, 1988 (Ken Kwapis, director; John Bailey, cinematographer; Carol Littleton, editor)
- *A Dry White Season*, 1989 (Euzhan Palcy, director)
- *Dimenticare Palermo*, 1990 (Francesco Rosi, director; Pasqualino De Santis, cinematographer)

- *Billy Bathgate*, 1991 (Robert Benton, director; Néstor Almendros, cinematographer)
- *Last of the Mohicans*, 1992 (Michael Mann, director; Dante Spinotti, cinematographer)
- *Nobody's Fool*, 1994 (Robert Benton, director; John Bailey, cinematographer)

Joan Jett and Michael Fox; *Light of Day*

Nestor Alemendros and me; *Places in the Heart*

Me, Lorraine Bracco, Herman ?, and Harvey Keitel

Robert Benton, Dustin Hoffman, and me; *Billy Bathgate*

On the Set of *Copkiller* and other 80s/90s Films • 143

Me and Stanley Tucci; *Billy Bathgate*

Me, Jeff Goldblum, John Bailey, Gabriele Lucci, Cyndi Lauper; *Vibes*

Cyndi Lauper and me in Ecuador, *Vibes*

Daniel Day-Lewis, Wes Studi, Jody May, and Steve Waddington, *Last of the Mohicans*

Larry Blyden

LARRY BLYDEN WAS A DEDICATED ACTOR who had a reputation for being loud, tough, irritating, and someone who was *not* loved by all. I'd known him for some time, but not well, and I remember not particularly liking him either. He had married the wonderful dancer, Carol Haney. They had two children, a boy and a girl. It was only after Carol's sad death—she was a serious diabetic, with an equally serious drinking problem who developed an illness untreatable by certain sulfa drugs—that Larry and I became friends.

He was a snappy dresser and seemed to own a zillion pairs of glasses that all seemed to be of the same design. They were thick-lensed with dark thick frames or wire frames. They were the aviator style that was the fad at the time. Larry was always working in some play or doing a musical. I think at this time he was in *The Norman Conquests*, running back and forth between two theaters.

One night we had a wild idea and wondered whether we should "do it." We thought about it, laughed, and then decided to make oatmeal cookies instead.

Larry was interested in everything and this is what I came to adore about him. He was a gifted actor, photographer, show host, and as time proved, a loyal friend. Again, *not* easy to work with.

One night Larry and my then-husband decided they would bake some key lime pies as Larry had just completed a cooking course and had arrived at our apartment with a sack of limes. Since there was no air conditioning in our kitchen and it was a hot summer night, I suggested that perhaps it was not such a grand idea to be baking that evening.

I was vetoed! I faded to another room in the apartment and decided to let them bond. After some time had passed, I simply couldn't repress the desire to see what they were up to. On my first pass, there they were standing there in their jockey shorts, sweat streaming down their bodies in rivulets. Larry, bespectacled, extended his arm as he lectured about breaking the egg and straining the egg whites through your fingers while the yolk remained in the palm. He had forgotten that a utensil of some kind to catch all of this would have been helpful.

I *flew* as I heard the *schplott*! I returned again a while later for the rolling of the pie crust. This time I was greeted by two white flour faces, blobs of dough everywhere, and one wide flat piece of dough resembling a large thin pizza that rested on the counter top.

Again, I flew.

At this time, Larry was about to start a wonderful new job for Mark Goodson—one that would allow him to make a great deal of money and give him exposure in reaching a huge audience. He decided to take a trip around the world before his stint was to begin. I (and the husband) received cards and gifts from Japan, India, and China. At one point he sent word he was on his way to Morocco. It was about that time that the phone rang to tell us that he had been in an accident. He was seriously hurt, but alive. Larry had been driving his rented car heading toward a village at the edge of the Sahara. It was never clear if something hit his car, or if it had gone out of control as his cameras and luggage were all intact.

Mark Goodson was preparing to send someone to bring him back to the states from Agadir, which is in the south of Morocco. He had been moved twice from one small station to another. Somehow he managed to get a phone call through which, believe me, is a near miracle in that part of the world. We believed the story we heard. The steering wheel had smashed into his chest, his spleen had been removed at some point, but he was all right and had sent love to his kids Ellen and Josh, and his mom. We also heard that he knew someone was going to fetch him.

Time passed and the difficulties began. This horror *began* because it was Ramadan, the highest of holy days in Morocco. Larry was in a remote place in the country and communication was just about impossible. The capital city is Rabat and all official buildings were closed.

Suddenly, it became quite another story when the Mark Goodson representative arrived. Larry Blyden was dead. This was followed by the news that he couldn't remove Larry's remains from the country, as the religious laws forbade it at that time. Finally, after many concerned telephone calls, we got to Mr. Henry Kissinger, who as usual waved a few magic wands and Larry Blyden's body was sent back to the states. Ben Edwards, the stage designer and a dear friend of Larry's and my ex, went to identify the body. Larry was to be cremated and his mother would take his ashes home. The day of the funeral, I bought huge bouquets of field flowers consisting of poppies, blue delphiniums, daisies, and Queen Anne's lace —a very American look—to place near his coffin at Riverside Chapel. After the short ceremony, quite suddenly there was a rumble, and everything began to move like the ascent of a rollercoaster. The casket, the flowers—we were each to take a flower to keep in his memory—everything disappeared. And all at once it was all over.

The effect was stunning!

Later that day, I sat on my terrace conversing with Larry's mother and his aunt. "Larry is looking down on us," I said to them. "I feel him so close, don't you?" A fierce wind suddenly appeared and ripped the large, heavy awning off its frame. Oh yeah, Larry was with us, indeed!

He was curious about so many things. Dying at that time was definitely something that did not pique his interest. His girlfriend, Laura, who had traveled with him (none of us even knew about her) insisted that he wear his favorite black velvet jacket and she took great care selecting his tie.

There was a kind of wake later on at his apartment. As his friends were embracing the family who were getting ready to leave—they had been there a long time—a woman arrived. She came, as she confessed, 'at her usual time,' carrying a box of Danish pastries. She had been a sex partner of Larry's, and she wistfully reminded me that 'her hot sex cream' still remained at the side of his bed. She was so touched!

That Larry was a devil, he was—and full of surprises.

On Teaching

ONE DAY STELLA ADLER CALLED ME in a seductive tone and led me to believe that she had something juicy for me.

"I'd like you to teach style for me. You see, darling, no one has it," she said. "Come, we'll discuss it when you come to lunch; that is if someone…makes it!"

I can't remember if I was out of work at that time, but the *master* had called. I was reverent and thrilled at the same time. For me, there has never been a teacher *and* mentor in my life with the power and intellect to equal Stella's. She filled me with the desire to leave my small world and see everything wherever I could. To read, go to museums, study, travel—anything and everything—to grow. If you studied with her, however, you did it *her* way.

There are many who accused her, as a teacher, of being cruel to women students, but she was never so to me. Nor did I witness her being cruel to students when I studied with her. However, there are too many who attest to this happening so it must have been true for some. She adored talent, and beautiful people with courage. She whetted my senses and my curiosity. "Plays are about ideas!" she claimed. Her words stay with me and ignite my brain. Even now she has my 'ear.'

"*Good* plays are about *ideas*."

So she told me that she wanted me to teach style and this would include the movement, the dances, and the manners of the time.

"I want you to teach, Sondra."

I then asked, "What scripts do you want me to give to the students to work on? "

"*None* darling," she said. I do *not* want you to *speak* to them."

"Stella, I laud you, but that is impossible. And I do *not* want to teach dance class or movement class since that holds no interest for me. Stella, just this once trust me. Let me do it my way, your way, and let me *speak*!"

That was the beginning of a ten-plus year working relationship.

"I'll give you a place to always be working in and of the theatre—it's where you belong. I'm giving you a *base*," she said. I became the highest paid, underpaid teacher at Stella's school.

Salaries were not Stella's best thing. She never let you teach more then a few hours a week. When her husband, Mitchell Wilson, the physicist and writer died, she asked me to take over her classes for the time she was away, which I did. I began to teach almost anything that dealt with acting, in any manner I thought was of value as time went by. Often, Stella would come and sit in on my classes, and I would often return to her classes as well.

Stella's script breakdown classes were stunningly astute. Arthur Miller, Shaw, Ibsen, Williams. Stella came from Yiddish theatre royalty, the famed Group Theater. Stella went to study with Stanislavsky. She analyzed those plays and understood the larger themes so that the actor really understood what the playwright was saying, and cleared the way for the actor to put the text into acting terms with the director. Stella taught me to love teaching actors to do the play.

I am seduced by talent. I once complained to Stella about Brando's destructive behavior with his wives and children. Stella said, "Darling, he doesn't have to be *good*."

I'm not sure this is a reality. Nor do I feel that if you're a good man, a good girl, a good person, that you should necessarily be guaranteed 'good' reviews.

The bits and pieces of a life make a whole person—a whole picture—don't try to give them a form.

Sometimes It Happens

WHEN I RETURNED FROM PLAYING *Hello, Dolly!* in Vietnam, Stella and Bobby Lewis were teaching at Yale. Stella approached me about teaching with them there, and arranged a meeting with Robert Brustein, Dean of the Drama Department. During that time the phone in his office kept ringing with frequent interruptions from this guy who would eventually become my husband. He had started the Long Wharf Theatre with *Jon Jory* and was so threatened by the *possibility* that I might join them at Yale that it further fermented his dislike for Brustein. Of course, I didn't know any of this at the time.

Later that afternoon it was announced on the radio that Martin Luther King had been shot and killed. The effect upon me was staggering since I had just returned from that sea of violence in Vietnam. I rode the train back to Manhattan with Stacy Keach who was in the company at Yale, both of us in a state of disbelief. We didn't exchange more than a few solemn words. Ultimately, I was so disturbed that I passed on the Yale offer to both teach and appear with the company. Instead, I quickly left for the south of France, needing the comfort of my family of friends.

In France I received *exactly* what I needed most. So when the *guy* from the Long Wharf arrived, I asked him what he was doing in the south of France. He said he was *following* me! Well, that was flattering! He was producing a show in New York and he came all the way to France to come get me.

front row: Jeanne Moreau with her dog, Quick, me, Francois Truffaut; second row: Jean-Claude Vignes, Tan, Karla, Jeanne's father, Jean Louis Richard (Jeanne's first husband), Lou Lou; Jeanne's house in La Moure

WOW. I was bowled over. I went on with my plans and proceeded to my next stop, Paris. This is where he proposed. I was overwhelmed, flattered, and needy. Without thinking, I said *yes* and promptly walked into the headlights of an oncoming taxi!

I should have known it was a sign.

A larger accident to follow.

The marriage was doomed. I found out his plan ten years later. All along, his intent was to marry me and leave me in ten years, *after* he had met all my friends and peers in the theatre!

But that is another story about big lessons to be learned.

A Few Bumps in the Road

MY RELATIONSHIPS IN THE PAST WERE COMPLICATED. I followed a pattern, especially with married men. I was comfortable being *favorite child*, but I'd often find myself in big trouble in this role. If I slept with a best friend's husband, it wasn't because I particularly wanted to, but because I found myself confronted by someone that provoked the situation. Although I'm a fairly perceptive person when it comes to others, I've always felt that my own self-judgment was bad because I had such childlike needs. Once I was sitting on my bed with an actor friend who was married. We were rehearsing a scene. All of a sudden he said, "Well, how do we do this?"

"Excuse me?" I said, not getting it at all.

"Sondra, we are not on a *beach*." My bed...a beach? I hadn't thought about the incident as anything but a rehearsal.

It seems I've had misconceptions and made mistakes in the past and paid an enormous price. The longest relationships I've had have been with male and female *friends*. These friendships have had a great sense of continuity in my life and I find enormous comfort in them. I work better and freer; I am excited by the intellectual exchange of ideas. For me, one of the most pleasing aspects of friendship is the creative exchange—to share information about new writers, plays, painters, and composers.

On Husbands

I MUST HAVE BEEN NAIVE OR TOO TRUSTING about the men I married. The first—Sidney Armus—was an actor and a wonderful one, appearing in such productions as *Mr. Roberts, South Pacific,* and *Wish You Were Here*. He was a little crazy, but dedicated to his art. I'm sure our confusion as to what constituted a marriage had nothing to do with reality. We had fun at first, yet soon entered different forms of transferences that seemed to have more to do with our analysts than with each other. Coming from a disciplined theatre life was one thing, but we didn't understand what commitment or intimacy in a relationship really meant.

back row: Robert Rauschenberg, Jasper Johns, Roland Pease; middle row: Grace Hartigan, Mary Abbot, Steve Rivers, Larry Rivers, Herbert Machiz, Tibor de Nagy, John Myers; front row: Joe Hazan, Maxine Grofsky, me (standing), Jane Freilicher (photo credit: John Gruen)

The reward of applause or praise didn't reassure me, nor did the men I chose to marry. When my second marriage was faltering, I began to study painting, which was not a giant step, as I had grown up in an environment with painters. The New York School of Painters and Poets was emerging—Larry Rivers, Robert Rauschenberg, Jasper Johns, Grace Hartigan, Jane Wilson, Mary Frank, Willem de Kooning, and many more.

I began to have shows of my paintings and sculpture.

Painting by me

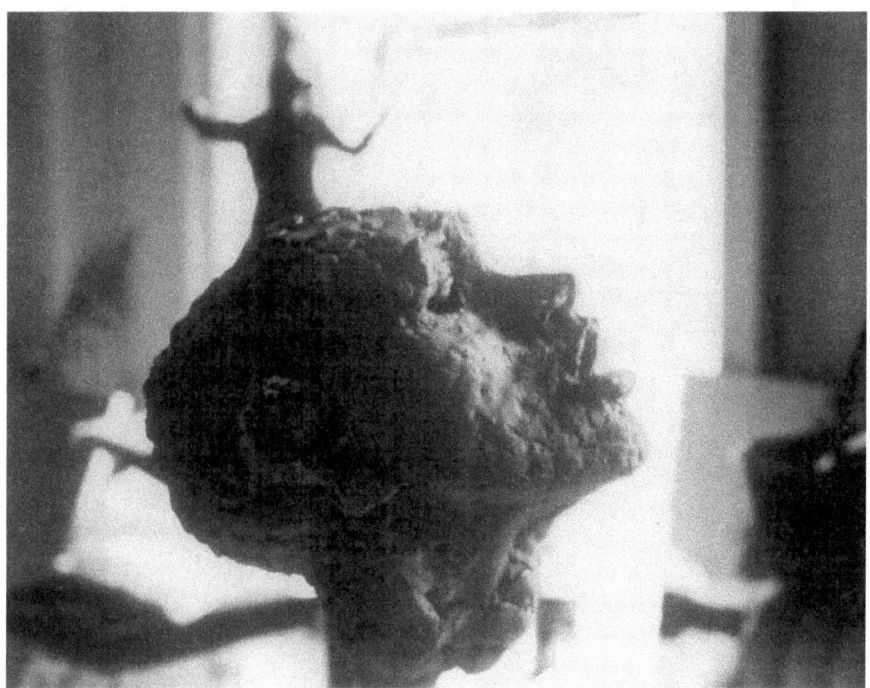

Ceramic head by me

I always knew I could sing for my supper but thought I was not entitled to much more. Just don't ask for more and don't question anything. Low self-esteem. If I flirted or sent up signals, I was not aware of consciously doing so. I somehow thought if my boyfriends were enamored of me, it must have been because I was exciting on the stage. So I had to be good in bed. Listen, why argue?

More on Relationships

IN RETROSPECT, I THINK THE UNIONS that inspired my violence and despair came from my marriages. When my sense of futility and rage were left festering too long, I would explode, blindly striking out, in a suicidal way aiming at myself, breaking glass, swallowing pills, slashing wrists. Dramatic, yes. Immature, I was told, and I agreed. But a cry for help! I went into analysis for long periods of time.

Through the years I have lived more creatively, more calmly, alone. I feel safer in my own hands. It has been a bumpy road to this time in my life.

Back to the lesson of *teaching!*

Teaching has been a long journey for me. Studying with teachers such as Stella Adler, Robert Lewis, Lee Strasberg, and a bit with the Canadian director, John Hirsch, I was able to develop a spectrum of the wisdom from some of our masters in the acting teaching profession.

Although teaching acting does not translate into a huge fortune *monetarily,* my riches have been to see some of my actors really soar. Some are loyal and loving for years after they get there; some forget me. But it is a joy for me and I am proud of the work we have done and the trust that lasts for years. To aid actors to find themselves—to allow them to find their own *voice*, to honor the playwright, to help them be fearless in their approach to the journey they must *all* take—gives me such pride. I have actively been in many aspects of the arts for many years now. I know how qualified a good teacher must be. Most importantly, you must top your own background and love—love what you do.

It can be dangerous to teach if you're not really qualified. There are people who do it in order to add to their income, or because they like the idea of being some kind of a 'guru.' And then there are those who love to prey on troubled younger actors, and are looking for new bed partners. (I'm not fooling!) These people anger and disgust me.

I begin to think of the time that gets wasted. Learning the craft of acting takes TIME. The talent you are born with must be nurtured and enlightened. To work on your craft takes bravery, talent, and again—TIME. It's a process; don't let anyone kid you. From time to time, I've been amused to hear a famous model (nearly past her prime) say, "Well I guess I'll act now." Then I ask, "How long did it take for you to become the model you are today?" The answer more often will be, "Oh a few years." Then I ask, "Do you have a few *more* you're willing to spend? "

Accepting the responsibility of teaching is like being a surgeon. You have to be very careful not to handle someone's innards lightly or capriciously, for this can be dangerous, harmful, and damaging. Even the vibe in the room can be felt in a teaching situation. Although the actor usually can rehearse almost anywhere, I find it advantageous to create a healthy environment to teach in.

A good actor is a very astute observer. So much about a character one creates is behavioral—the way they physically respond to situations, large or small. Many actors like to read biographies. The life of a person contains the different events that have shaped their character or the lack of it. Their habits and choices become part of who they are. It affects their choices. An actor's *CHOICES* are an actor's talent.

Soul-searching is painful, and often *anger*-making. Very often the actor will locate events in their lives that release angry feelings, and then have to exhibit them for all to see. Yet this often painful journey allows them the *permission* to apply these feelings to the work. To really go to their dark—and even darkest—side. It's not particularly pleasant but rather courageous and upsetting.

The director creates psychology into behavior. The events in the play inform the audience what is happening but it all stems from the text. And underneath the text, more importantly is the *spine*.

Why are you —the character—telling me this?

Who has the secret?

What is it *really* like when it happens?

Why did the playwright put this scene in the play?

There's a part of the actor that sits on your own shoulder and observes, that comments as you rage, age, bleed, or laugh. And then catalogues the material. It shows up later in a theme, a song, a character, a poem.

It gets *used*.

When my dog, Molly, was dying after having lost eight puppies she had just given birth to, I remember how I cried. It was in a voice that was so animal in its grief. And as I heard this strange sound emitting from my throat, when there are no tears left, a part of me that sat on my shoulder said, "This is the *Greeks*! This is how to play Greek tragedy!"

The actor learns not to make up thoughts and meanings that aren't logical in terms of the play or the character. Natural is not real in terms of the theatre. Tension is misplaced energy. You stop yourself from doing something because you're frightened, because you want so badly to do it well. The actor must *commit*. Acting is *doing*. And what we *do* conditions how we speak. Often I announce, "Don't work with just one partner in class, or in life!"

I tell you, it's thrilling and scary as you become more and more aware that show business *is* a business—a big one. And the stakes are getting higher and higher!

Show business is a business! Good acting is an art!

On the Set of Billy Bathgate

WHILE CONSULTING FOR ROBERT BENTON on his film, *Billy Bathgate,* Tim Jerome, one of the actors, asked me if he could bring his little daughter to the set in order to meet "Tiger Lily," the character I played on stage and in the TV version of *Peter Pan* with Mary Martin. Of course I delightedly agreed.

So here comes this little adorable, blonde, blue-eyed, innocent, peachy-skinned child, and her excited Dad who is completely sure that making this introduction will insure a place in that young heart forever.

The proud Papa got down on one knee and said, "Sweetheart, this is Tiger Lily."

She gazed up at me and I gazed down at her, but what we expected was not exactly what we got! Her hands shot up to her cheeks, her eyes filled with the shocked look of someone stunned by a horrific accident.

Aghast, she cried, "WHAT HAPPENED??"

Finally, after what seemed to be the longest time, Tim decided that fatherly wisdom was apropos. "Darling, when we get older, things happen."

Aging

"**Death is nature's way of telling you to slow down.**"
Who said this?
I can't remember. I think *Anonymous* said it.
But just in terms of aging, when it hits, it hits a hard blow.
Colette said a test was to pull the skin on your hand and if the return was slow, not springing back, it was a sign that age was *here to stay* and would only get worse.

Dancers have always been nonverbal, as a rule; they're taught to articulate with their bodies and rarely express themselves as easily in other forms. It is hard for them to make the transition from dancing to speaking roles and many have been smokers in past years. What amazes me is how often dancers become drinkers. When a dancer suspected their dancing days might be over, they tended to smoke or drink *a lot*. I recall going to a reunion at Jerry Robbins' house and two-thirds of the dancers in the room were in AA.

Yet I think the most courageous people in the arts *are* dancers because dancers know the life span they have is so limited. Early injuries can threaten their lives and this is something a dancer must take responsibility for. Yet the joy of dancing *far* exceeds any of the trials. Although I must say, I have not known many dancers who have actually 'planned ahead.' For you just don't see it coming and you just don't want to *accept* what is happening. Aging.

The sadness I have when seeing faces I used to know, so very pulled, the lips go ear to ear—I've seen it so many times. They say most Hollywood faces are on the cutting room floor, and that's no joke. The amount of face-lifts, peelings, botox, and corrective surgery just to maintain a sense of youth not fading is judged by some as necessary. "I've had some work done." That's how we now put it. I'll hear someone say, "I only had a mini-lift." *Only a* mini-lift? Me too!

Some of us think we need to be with an extremely handsome man or woman, or a younger person, in order to feel beautiful or desirable. I've been drawn to persons younger, older, beautiful, and gifted because I'm used to it. Willa Kim, the brilliant designer, and I were complaining to one another believing that the men we should be seeing aren't young. As a matter of fact, they seem decrepit. We agreed we're accustomed to being around beautiful people.

Change is inevitable; and the prospect both scares me and excites me. The south of France, where I've spent many of my best times, has no right to change. And yet it does, as we all do. I look at the swollen knees and malformed feet of dancers after years of abuse and overwork and over-extending, and I'm so deeply touched.

It's strange but even at this age, I've always thought of most of my friends as being older than me. They all assume ("Never assume," says Jay Julien, my lawyer!) some familial role— mother, father, aunt, uncle, brother, or sister. Recently a friend said to me, "You're younger than I am."

I replied, "I am not."

She said, "I *know* that. But you *seem* like you are."

Perhaps many feel that I'm younger because when I *was* younger, I believed they'd all take care of me. This is what I thought—"He or she knows what to do, so I'm saved! They will protect me." Where that concept came from, I have no idea. I really do not know, but I have it even now. And when I'm disappointed by someone it can be because they have said to me, "*You* take care of this now" or worse, "No! You must take care of this." I find myself conflicted for a time, although I know better, that they are right and mean me no harm. I find most people in the arts are afflicted in much the same way: their view of themselves is childlike.

The resistance to *take care of things* is enormous. Surviving in the arts is so very draining that we are drawn to people and situations where we feel there may be a respite from the stress.

We often give ourselves over to managers, agents, lawyers, hairdressers, makeup artists, directors—you name it! If it means a sense of protection, or being taken care of, we go there. Sometimes it can become a long line of Lemmings!

I'm at the age now that forces me to see *more* clearly what age is about. Sometimes I will see an actor, dancer, or writer that I haven't seen in a long time, and at times it's like the shock of seeing a piece of favorite porcelain or china fall and *smash*. There he or she is, alarmingly appearing so much older. Often the figure is thicker, sometimes porcine. That lovely lean, lithe body of the past is no longer, or even vaguely, the same. That bubble above and below the belt line. The vibe that used to exude vitality is energy-less, missing.

Back in the 1980s, on a particular New Year's Eve, Jerry Stiller and Anne Meara gave an extravagant, huge party that they refer to as "that one great money year we had!!" Well, the guests just kept arriving—by taxis, subways, buses, giant stretch limos—it was really something! I overheard this joyous remark. "*Sweetheart, Bubalah!* Oh my God, I'm so happy to see you again. I THOUGHT YOU WERE DEAD!"

Time takes its toll. Life takes its piece as well. There are dancers and actors that I've known from the past that are almost unrecognizable and yet there are others that have remained pretty much the same. Well, maybe a size larger. The skin is healthy and tight, maybe a few lines, but the body attitude is strong, the aura is alive and illuminated with a light.

Arthritis is a cruel ailment. To a dancer, it's the meanest cut of all. It's such a crippler but the body still *knows* what it was capable of *before*. Nothing can change that. When I was in *Ballets U.S.A.*, I ruptured my Achilles tendon and suffered great trauma. It was never the same for me again. Mentally, I have never totally recovered. Joyously I joined John Butler's Company and returned to Spoleto for the second year. But I never totally recovered. However, you can still keep up your *will*, your diet, your spirit. You must love!

Actors have the most difficult time with aging, having to accept playing characters that are older than the concept they have of themselves. It's often the women that have the roughest time accepting the jump from ingenue to Mama or from leading lady to Granny. Even when accepting this reality, one finds oneself *still* not being cast and hired, and becomes devastated and feels abandoned. Bette Davis took out an ad in *Variety*, making it clear that she was a *star* looking for employment. She was certainly a 'piece of work.'

Marge Champion, whom I adore, has taught me more about coming to terms with the *scaries*. On her 80-something-th birthday, she had a celebration that was grand. She hosted a tea dance for two hundred people and invited a few dance teams, including her favorite partners—soup to nuts! She has learned to salute herself. And we salute her too. Marge, who was the model for *Snow White,* the Hippo for *Fantasia* for Walt Disney, and all those dancing films and TV shows with Marge and Gower Champion. Aw, come on!

Alice Esty was my friend who lived into her mid-90's. One late spring day, she gathered a group of composers and poets that she had championed at the beginning of their careers at her apartment. Alice had been one of the mentors of Francis Poulenc, Ned Rorem, Fizdale and Gold, among others. The voices, the music, the lyrics of John Ashbery, Kenneth Koch, Arnold Weinstein, Frank O'Hara, John Gruen were enjoyed by all who were there. The composers and poets of art songs were grateful to her for her help when they indeed needed it and she enjoyed having them all there at her side again. She was publicly reciting T.S. Eliot's *Quartet* at ninety-three years old and reading, painting, and enjoying her grandchildren. Her body didn't allow her to walk for even a few blocks without pain. She studied Tai Chi a few times a week and she would move her body in the most harmonious ancient way.

You know what pisses me off with growing older?

All right, I'll tell you.

It's when I'm feeling really good, and someone jumps up and offers me their seat in a crowded subway train. I *justify* their graciousness by telling myself, "It's because I'm so well dressed!" I mean, I still look pretty good, or so I'm told. After *talking* to a friend you haven't seen for a long time, they begin to look like they used to appear to you, don't they?

Don't they?

One afternoon, I ran into Arlette who was dancing in a ballet company at the time. She later moved to the south of France and taught dance at Rosella Hightower's. Her love of animals leaves her tending 25 cats or more. We waved to one another. She gingerly greeted me. "Are you staying at Number 8? Great! I'm fucking at number 10!"

* * *

From My Diary

PARIS, EARLY MAY,

Here I am again in Paris on a sunny day, still soaking up the nourishment of my past here. I'm staying at Tanya Lopert's apartment on the Rue Cassini, and locating old friends. I accompanied Tanya to her face massage lady on the Rue Francois Première. I left her there and was standing at the corner. Suddenly I found myself trembling, agitated. Something was happening to me. I rounded the corner and looked up to decide where I was. The street sign told me I was on the Rue Quentin Bauchart where Jean-Claude Vignes' family had that large rambling apartment—the one from the early days when we all first knew one another.

My being on this corner is not a mistake.

It is for some reason a refresher. A refresher to remember the people I have loved and lost. And how much time has gone by. I hate sounding artsy-fartsy about all this…but there you are.

The trees in Paris are that nervous, delicate green. I just had lunch with André Francois, the political cartoonist and painter, and his lovely wife, Margaret. They drove into Paris from Grisy-les-Plâtres in the foul and unusually cold, rainy weather for their region. He seems to be seriously depressed, which saddens me although it never seems to diminish his genius.

One Christmas Eve when they were in New York, I invited them to dinner. I was preparing what I thought would be a special French dinner for the three of us—a recipe I had never made before—Rognons de Veau. They brought a bottle of Lafite Rothschild wine to celebrate. I opened it to let it breathe and blithely poured the bottle into the kidney stew! They were stunned, but kept a straight face and gazed innocently ahead as if I had done nothing wrong by dumping all that glorious expensive wine into a searing pot of kidney stew.

We are now walking along the Boulevard as I head back towards Tanya's apartment. André is describing how this is the very street where he picked up Margaret years ago. He had been a young Romanian painter who chose France as his new country and she was a very young English girl. As we walk together I notice how white their hair is now. They are still generous, witty, adorable.

I should describe their house in the little village where they live. It is without a doubt a dream house. Much of it is trompe l'œil—an enchanted cottage! There is a room that has no windows but is flooded with light. At the painted windows little curious animals peer in—black deer noses pressed to the glass; inquisitive birds tapping at the windows. They have a collection of small toys and a bevy of amusing variations of all sorts of sardines! André's studio isn't far from the house. It's just below a little hill, nestled below the garden. There are a variety of fruit trees, vines, and country flowers and there's always something delicious to eat just coming out of the oven.

And now here I am walking with them, wanting to squeeze them for the joy of knowing them. I chuckle as I recall how I dumped that great vintage wine that night.

L'œuvre d'André François détruite
Tout a brûlé !
Illustrateur, peintre, sculpteur, cet artiste de 87 ans, connu dans le monde entier, a vu les flammes réduire à néant le travail d'une vie. Aujourd'hui ses amis se mobilisent

André's studio burned to the ground and all of his work in it was destroyed. The news of this disaster was reported in all the newspapers in Europe. He died a short time afterward.

Robbins Died at Twelve Noon

July 29, 1998: *New York Times*
ROBBINS DIED AT TWELVE NOON

WHEN GWIN JOH CHIN CALLED, the information had just reached the *New York Times* where she was at work as an editor of the magazine section. I had known that Jerry was quite frail for some months. I had a gnawing feeling that week that I should call him, kind of feeling that whispers in your ear, "Call Jerry, or write him a silly card." You know, that kind of thing.

Then Gwin asked if I had "heard."

"Heard what?"

A leaden beat went by. "Jerry died this afternoon."

I heard myself gasp and scream, "No, oh please, no!"

"There will be a memorial with the N.Y. City Ballet in the future," she reported. Blindly I ran from room to room in my apartment, wailing his name, holding my aching stomach. I kept stroking my hair, repeatedly smoothing it, trying to make order of some kind. My innards seemed to have exploded.

I dialed Jerry's line at home. A young woman's voice answered: it might have been Kathy. "Is what I have just heard so? Please tell me, I know Jerry really well, I'm not a…uh, uh." I didn't know what I was. "I'm Peanuts—that's what he called me…Sondra. It's Sondra, I don't know if you know me."

Her voice was gentle and patient. "Of course I know you. I want to reassure you he died without pain, surrounded by people who he cared for and they for him. His sister Sonia, Brian, and Jerry's dog, Tessie, were with him, and he went quietly."

I could hardly hear her any more. I asked, "Is Sonia, Jerry's sister, there?"

"Yes, she's with him now." She suggested I give her my number and Sonia would call me later when she had the chance. I gave her my number. "Please don't hang up, not just yet, please just keep talking to me for a while." I couldn't bear to break the connection. It was like an umbilical cord. I was so sure he would come on the line as usual with "Hi, what's up?" and giggle. I began to get emotional and vague, thanked her, and hung up the phone.

In less then five minutes Sonia returned my call. Her voice was calm and loving. "Why don't you come over and see him." It was then that I realized he was at home, there in his house.

"I have to teach class from four until six thirty." I felt too helpless.

"Come after class, we should be here until nine for sure."

"Thank you, thank you for the honor, Sonia."

"You should be here; you're like family."

I prepared for class, thinking, "I must not spoil this last class of the season for my acting students; it could be a shambles." Donna Hanover arrived at the same time as I. She had a driver who picked her up after class. "Please, Donna, can you help me? Could it be possible for you to drop me at the East Side, someone close to me has died." Of course she offered her assistance. The scenes went brilliantly, everyone was prepared, and anxious to work. I felt such pride and gratitude. Just every once in a while my patience ran short. I tried to keep myself in check. After the final scene, I made my way to the center of the small stage space, trembling, and tried to keep control. "Can we have a minute of silence? Today a great man of the theatre has died." As I said the name Jerome Robbins, I lost it and began to weep. "The genius of Jerome Robbins has left us. The last of the masters is gone." Silence followed.

Donna's car dropped me at the house. I sprinted toward the house and pushed the bell. The door opened swiftly. It was Kathy at the entrance. I recognized her voice, not her face. Her clothes were simple, a yellow tee shirt and a navy short skirt. She wore an apron. "They're upstairs; go on up."

Passing the office on the ground floor, I proceeded up a flight of stairs; the walls are a warm buttery yellow. To the left is a small dining room. It's a wonderful red. A bay window faces a green lush garden below. Just outside the window is a small balcony filled with plants. Everything looked just as it always did; the dog was stretched out on the floor snoozing. There were four or five people seated in the dining area on gold delicate Victorian chairs. My eyes panned them as I went by into the room. There on the table was a tray of thin elegant sandwiches of salmon, chicken, egg salad, small cakes, and white and red wine. I saw Buzz Miller seated along with Sonia's son, daughter, and Sonia's husband, George Cullenin. Suddenly Sonia was there, looking calm, centered, no shoes, barefoot, wearing a light blue denim skirt and shirt. Her hair was silver-gray and shorter than I remembered.

"Eat something, in a little while there will be nothing left."

The power in her eyes was the same. She hugged me and held me affectionately. I hung on to her like a life raft. "Then you go up and see him."

There were a few there I recognized. I had a glass of red wine and then motioned to Sonia that I was ready to see Jerry. "Come." She gestured her head toward the upstairs. She tapped lightly and Brian opened the door and allowed us in.

The bedroom was the same as always. The light was soft—not eerie or sad. The old wrought iron headboard, half painted white and half-brass. In a three-quarter bed, lay the figure of Jerry, peaceful as Sonia had said, lying in the center of his bed. He appeared to be smaller, delicate, slightly barrel-chested. As I gazed at him, the aura was serene. Jerry was wearing the same bridegroom's shirt from *Les Noces*, his ballet recently revived by N.Y. City Ballet. A coral color crepe-like fabric with a trim of a lighter color at the standing neck and cuffs of the sleeves. I remembered it so well it from his ballet—so Russian.

There at his left shoulder was the tiny nosegay of white blossoms the bridegroom wears in the ballet. Grey blue jeans (he would have really loved that). And then I said something lame like, "His socks match his shirt. That's good. No shoes." Sonia kept touching his feet with little healing squeezes. His arms were folded on the lower part of his chest. In his beautiful hands rested a single white rose, which at its heart was pale green. I saw a glow about his head, his face, serene, but for a narrow band of cloth from below his jaw to the top of his head to keep the lower jaw from dropping. His beard sparkling white. Just the lips seemed ready to widen into a broader smile, there was a hint of it. A sliver of his front teeth was visible. Seeing him in his bed—so peaceful. Viewing him like this in his bed, in his room. Being taken from the hospital to the home he loved, to die. It was the best move for Jerry. I am sure it helped him more easily on his journey. I was told it took hours of negotiating by Sonia to arrange it this way.

"Darling Jerry, if it wasn't for you I probably wouldn't be here. I wouldn't have had the rewarding wonderful life I have had."

I'd ring him up and say, " Hey Jer, you wanna hear a funny sound?" He would giggle and giggle. This time there will be a long, long silence.

Jerome Robbins (photo credit: Martha Swope)

The following morning as Jerry's body was taken to be cremated—as he had wished—Brian told me the *New York Times* was being delivered to his home. His picture was on the front page announcing his passing; they passed each other.

"To die must be a very big adventure."
– Peter Pan

From the Corner of My Eye

I AM SEEING AMID THE OLD GOOD LUCK TELEGRAMS, invitations, playbills, expired passports, reviews, obits—in this seemingly bottomless box of mine—two letters neatly tied with a narrow green silk ribbon. I shall read them again. Odd that they are both signed JANE. One I can see is from the movie star, Jane Fonda. I had coached her on a movie, *The Morning After*, and came to respect her dedication to really doing the work. (She is also a terrific human being.) The second is from Jane Fleiss, a gifted hard-working actress. She had been a student of mine who has now become a fine acting teacher.

JANE FONDA

Dear Sondra,

It can't be easy for you and it's not easy for me, to know the remuneration and acknowledgement others will receive when YOU have already made such a creative and generous contribution to this film.

Please accept this as a token of what your contribution represents. I hope our work together will never have to be done under these circumstances again, and please know when the time comes (unless I fall on my face) I will let everyone know what you have done for me. It's been a real pleasure. I've learned a lot.

You are an impressive woman. I hope I can play some role in the realization of your dreams.

Give them hell in Chicago...But don't burn any bridges... Know what I mean?

GERONIMO!

JANE

(I was instructed to open this letter on the plane on the way back to New York and a check for an extra $10,000 floated to the floor—a sorely needed gift.)

Monday, December 29, 2003

Dearest Sondra,

I was absolutely shocked and saddened to read in this morning's paper of the death of Alan Bates.

I know you knew him very well and that he used to crash at your house between his brilliant performances in the Turgenev play.

I miss you so very much. I miss your class—the safest haven for an actor to work out in on the whole planet—please quote me on that. There is not a day that goes by and I am not indebted to you for your support of my life in the theatre, and your inspiration to me.

Actors act—it's that simple—that's what you always said. And you encouraged me to have a life outside the work, reassuring me that one's talent cannot be lost or misplaced, that one can always pick up the work again and get back to the joy of the pure craft of acting.

How I love you.

I am so sorry that you lost a friend and we lost another wonderful working actor,

All my love,
Janie Fleiss

What does all of this represent?
I will tell you.

A Life in the Arts

I CANNOT SAY THAT PEOPLE IN THE ARTS can't work it out. Yet the levels of rejection, frustration, humiliation and low self-esteem make it difficult to survive when you know in your heart of hearts that you are gifted.

Is it about winning or creating drama in order to be noticed and approved of? Is it about applause and public approval? What a truly schizoid, crazy existence. If you paint, you have to exhibit. If you write, someone has to read it. If you perform, someone else has to see you.

It is the sense of *community*—knowing that a *community exists*.

This has been the single largest appeaser and nourisher for most of us. This life. This wonderful life in the arts.

It is what has kept me going and why …

…I will keep going.

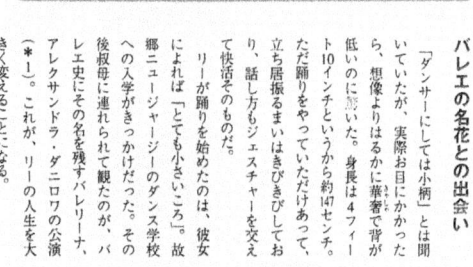

ブロードウェイ・レジェンド――プロの神髄 ⑦

BROADWAY LEGENDS PART 1

Sondra Lee
ソンドラ・リー［ダンサー、演技コーチ］

取材・文＝中島薫

バレエの名花との出会い

「ダンサーにしては小柄」とは聞いていたが、実際お目にかかったら、想像よりはるかに華奢で背が低いのに驚いた。身長は4フィート10インチというから約147センチ。ただ踊りをやっていうから約147センチ。立ち居振るまいはきびきびしており、話し方もジェスチャーを交えて快活そのものだ。

リーが踊りを始めたのは、彼女によれば「とても小さいころ」。故郷ニュージャージーのダンス学校への入学がきっかけだった。その後叔母に連れられて観たのが、バレエ史にその名を残すバレリーナ、アレクサンドラ・ダニロワの公演（＊１）。これが、リーの人生を大きく変えることになる。

Photo credit: Kaoru

Last Words

It's really great to have an extended family all over the world. Remember I told you I was a regular runner away-er? Well now, it's not from confusion, insecurity, or fear of abandoned ambition. It's just travel, travel, travel! Countries, cities, villages, sights, smells, different cultures, customs, mysteries—lessons to be learned. All intoxicating for me...

In truth, I haven't told so many of the stories and experiences I've had in these pages. There's so much more to tell.

But hear me.

All artists, especially when they're younger and starting out, are...oh, yes...competitive, crazy, troubled, destructive, seductive, needy, talented. They are also aware of each other, protective, caring, and view each other's work candidly. They take care of each other as best they can. They eat together, cook together, laugh, rehearse, study together, drink, and sleep together...like a room full of PUPPIES! Puppies!

*Hence the title of this book—**I've Slept With Everybody**.*

They say there's nothing like a good book...

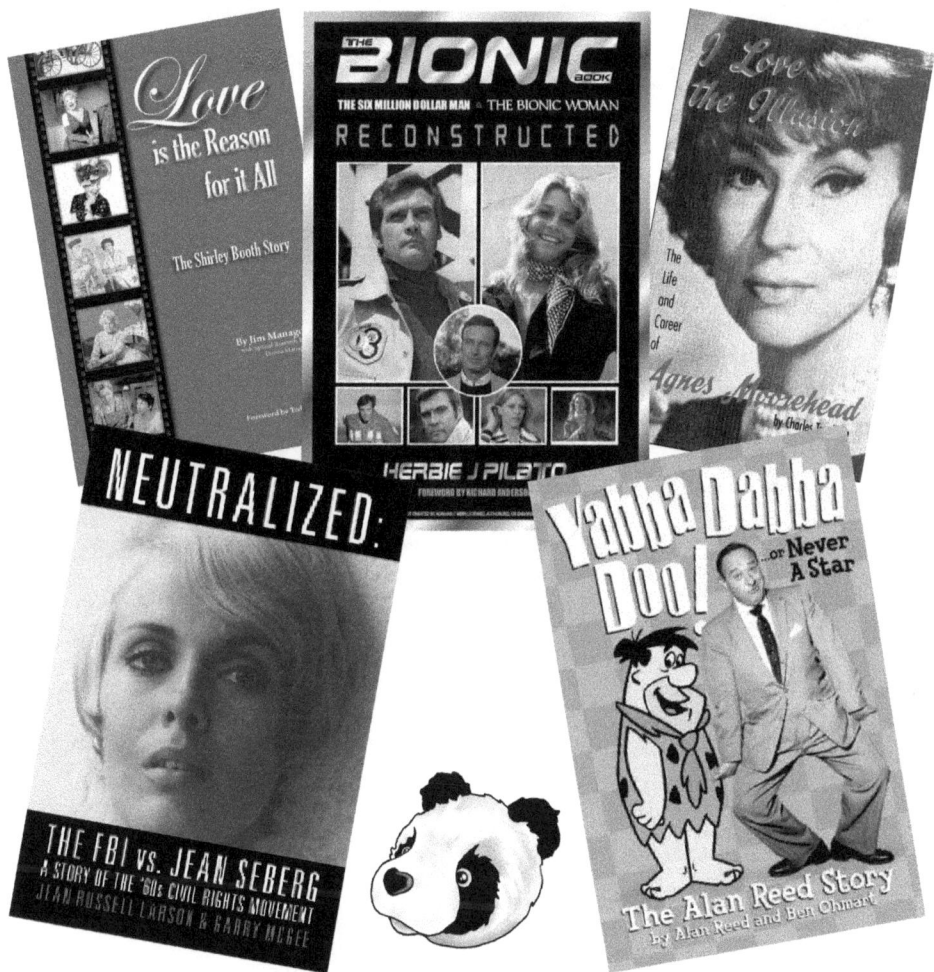

We think that says quite a lot!
BearManorMedia

P O Box 71426 • Albany, GA 31708
Phone: 760-709-9696 • Fax: 814-690-1559
Book orders over $99 always receive FREE US SHIPPING!
Visit our webpage at www.bearmanormedia.com
for more great deals!

www.ingramcontent.com/pod-product-compliance
Lightning Source LLC
Chambersburg PA
CBHW050803160426
43192CB00010B/1620